The Quiet Churches of Sussex

By Nigel C Winter

Also by the author

Travelling with Mr Turner

'Guide books will tell you that something is in the 'debased' style, meaning that it was built in the sixteenth, seventeenth or eighteenth centuries, but it does not matter when it was built or whether it is 'pure' or 'debased'. What does matter is, do you like the look of it yourself?'

John Betjeman
BBC broadcast
November 1948

Preface

I was drawn to the Church by its welcoming glow, one Autumn evening. I suspect that I was like so many commuters who made their way that night, in simply wanting to get home.

My day had been spent glaring at a bright computer screen and it was therefore a relief to log off and find myself under the rapidly darkening November skies.

I had walked past the Church as part of my daily commute for years. On the rare occasions that I was able to leave work early, I might have caught a glimpse of the verger scurrying through the archway as the double doors swung behind her. On a bad day I might contemplate how peaceful a time she'd had, amongst the still arches of the 13th century building, complying with little more than the gentle demands of occasional parishioners. Perhaps vergers didn't have to answer perpetually vibrating phones hidden about their distinctive attire.

Leaves danced across the flagstone entrance as I spied the empty pews in the shadows. I only step through the archway on a Sunday, I said to myself. Even so, I felt drawn to this most peaceful setting. I paused, unsure of the format. I have always been prone to letting myself down, so perhaps I could sit out of sight and just contemplate a while? Perhaps not, as the verger lit a candle on the font, illuminating precisely where I planned to hide.

Of course, there are Churches everywhere. There always have been. They are simultaneously a time capsule, sanctuary and of course places of worship. We are always going to them…next Sunday. Or at Christmas.

Was it evensong, evening prayer or evening psalms and what was the difference? I cautiously opened the door, mindful of any passing verger who might be tempted to waft down the aisle and dispense Bible readings to the unsuspecting. I am sure they know exactly how to make you find it hard to say 'no'. But all was hushed and very gently the day's tribulations started slowly slipping from my thoughts.

Placing myself in the choir stalls I noticed that two beady eyes were looking up at me from the seats below.

'We do all the odd numbers!' came the firm instruction from the tiny but redoubtable old lady to whom the eyes belonged.

'Excuse me?' I said quietly.

'The odd numbers. They …' she added with equal firmness and a flick of the head in the direction of the choir stalls opposite ' …do all the even numbers'.

Hush returned, but I was none the wiser. And then without instruction the four of us quietly recited the psalms in the old hymn book we'd been handed. It had been a ritual played out for an eternity, the very gentle mutterings of devotion in an increasingly noisy world. Sometimes I did the odd numbered paragraphs and sometimes both. But thankfully no one felt the need to break from their contemplation, to whisper a gentle admonishment, as we sat before the alter, bathed in the shadows cast by the gently flickering candles.

We possibly have a rather funny relationship with churches, I think. People openly question their relevance in an age when most 'answers' of some sort are available 'online'. We cherish them like we cherish institutions we don't really support. Institutions that make us feel good about our national identity, whilst privately concluding them an eccentric irrelevance; BBC Radio 3, the Tate Modern or Tunbridge Wells. Our patronage is scarce, but woe betide anyone who tries to take them away. But there is something more about Churches. There are over 10,000 medieval churches alone, all constructed when the population numbered less than 4 million. Clearly motivated by unwavering belief, they constructed churches before many had homes for themselves. Most contain artwork aged somewhere between 500 and 1000 years and yet we don't pay a penny to enter them. Generation upon generation were christened, married and ultimately buried around them. In many cases they are the one strong constant in the lives of the locality. And when as individuals or a nation we come upon the one great challenge that our logical scientific minds can neither solve or guarantee, we finally fill them. On the days around D-Day churches both sides of the channel were packed, and not always by the entirely faithful, but also by those that felt drawn, almost as a last resort, to beg for an outcome that in the darkest hour that only one could provide. Small wonder we revere them, when we are not walking past them, taking them for granted, as I did that November night.

Spiritual, aesthetic, historic, artistic, and once the original courts of justice, conveyors of literacy and rudimentary education; we are whom we are, because of our churches. Indeed, if we'd never had them or ever cease to have them, then we would cease to be who we are. But for the most part, they are just there, as they have always been there. Or as the poet Philip Larkin once wrote: -

Another church, matting seats and stone,
And little books; sprawlings of flowers, cut
For Sunday, brownish now; some brass and
stuff
Up at the holy end; the small neat organ;
And a tense, musty, unignorable silence…

I wondered if there might be more to these churches, and now seemed like a good idea to find out.

But which ones to choose?

I had an attraction to those Churches that were off grid, like Wigginholt, the first we encounter in this book. They 'feel', for want of a better word, more tranquil. It is as if one can sense the devotions over a millennium, that electricity, broadband, and much else can not disturb. More practically, the distance from the 'grid' means that all maintenance is sympathetic and in keeping with the methods used by those who laid the churches foundations. Their location coincides with a remoteness born of its purpose having moved on with a migrating population. There are no peasants working the land and their issue have long been flung to the far corners of the globe. Their families have upped and left, their work carried out by machines, their homes had fallen to dereliction, before sinking beneath the soil, where once home fires burned. But their place of worship remains, as if shame prevented the remaining locals from allowing them to go the same way. Over the passage of time they seem bereft of a purpose, their fortunes fluctuate over the centuries as still the visitors vary from the curious to the devout. And this gives them a new purpose, in a world where it is increasingly difficult 'to get away from it'.

Then, I could choose them randomly. Or in accordance with religious festivals for some pre-existing books on churches deal with merely the architectural. And in list form too ' ...*the church has a spire and a convenient car cark*...'Perhaps not.

Then, it may be just more satisfying to turn my cycle wheels to the road and see what happens. Indeed, John Betjeman's dictum was to seek out churches that are worth 'cycling twelve miles in the rain to see'. This then, shall be the basis of my selection.

Peaceful reading.

Chapter One

Wiggonholt

'Are there any bell ringers?' came the query from the gap in the door, 'Oh well I'd better give it a pull myself'.

And with that a solitary bell tolled across the ancient marshland at Pulborough, calling the faithful to Epiphany. This, a 3pm service on the first Sunday in January, in the Wildbrooks benefice.

If a worshipper from a millennia ago set foot in that Church today, it would be instantly recognisable. Only this day it took no fewer than 30 candles to bathe us in their golden glow and illuminate the pages of *Hymns Ancient & Modern*, along with the *Common Book of Prayer*. The Church remains off grid and surrounded by the Pulborough Brooks wetlands which is under the custodianship of the RSPB as oppose to being a source of food, as they were when the Church made its first appearance in document form in 1195. In all probability, it had been a place of worship long before then. The Saxon settlement made its presence felt latterly with the discovery of two dugout canoes as well as many ancient flints.

We were welcomed by a lady stood beside the two candles under the arched porch. T'was she who broke the bad news about the absence of any formal bell ringers, but this is the heart of the countryside which calls for resourcefulness. That and the fact there was only a solitary bell rope to contend with, meant that the task ahead was not as arduous as it first appeared.

We stepped through in to the Church and made the congregation up to a dozen. The gas lamps cast their glow in to the corners where the candles couldn't reach, as we were ushered to the front of the Church. This was indeed a church of bat droppings and furniture polish as John Betjeman had once described in the opening to the 1958 *Collins Guide to English Parish Churches*. But nowhere does Wiggonholt appear, perhaps due to it's remoteness. Yet he could have been thinking about this very Church in the introduction when he wrote: -

'…still they stand the churches of England, their towers grey above billowy globes of elm trees, the red cross of St George flying over their battlements, the Duplex Envelope System employed for collections, schoolmistress at the organ, incumbent in the chancel, scattered worshippers in the nave…'[1]

But aesthetics aside, we were here for a service to mark Epiphany, when the three wise men followed a star that lead to the stable in which Jesus was born. The vicar disabused us of the fairy tale notion that they made their way over sand dunes, rippling in the sunset as their camels lumbered away, taking the strain out of the journey. After studying the sky at night (their wisdom is attributed in part to a knowledge of astronomy and astrology) they made their way in the depths of winter, despite the temptation to put off the journey until better weather later on. And so the organ was roused into life as we sang:-

As with gladness men of old
did the guiding star behold,
as with joy they hailed its light,
leading onward, beaming bright:

*so, most gracious Lord, may we
evermore your splendour see.*

The candles gently danced as their glow
reflected in the polished cross and candle
sticks on the altar. Overhead a flight of geese
honked as they gently glided on to the
wetlands and the sun hovered over the South
Downs, in the distance.

Circumstances would not have allowed
the first parishioners to view their situation
quite so sentimentally. The Churches
foundations were laid when peasantry was rife
and the nation's population numbered just
three million. Seldom has mankind been
without conflict and then was no exception.
The Romans had left their mark, with a Villa
built half a mile to the north east of the
church, which quite possibly came to a bloody
end in a fire, indicating unsettled times. The
Saxons left their own mark in giving
Wigonholt its name – 'holt' meaning
woodland, Wiggon, or Wicga being the Saxon
who owned it. And in due course the Norman
invasion lead to Wiggonholt coming under the
ownership of the Benedictine Abbey at
Fecamp, between Lehavre and Dieppe on the
northern coast of France.

I wondered how many times a priest had
stood in the pulpit and shared their thoughts

with the intimate group of parishioners gathered, on the uncertainties of the times through which they were living. That evening, at the foot of the Downs, it could not have been more peaceful, and yet the new decade had opened with grave concern about events unfolding in Iran and Iraq, the home of the three wise men. And days before that whole region, and possibly beyond had been disturbed as an Iranian General had been assassinated by America. The oil price 'spiked' and the media went into overdrive, and yet it all seemed so far away as the mist billowed over the South Downs and spilt onto the wetlands.

That and many other sermons had been heard by Christ, depicted walking on water in the stained-glass east window. That window dates from 1859, having been made by Powell & Sons. The central medallion is constructed with stained glass of violet, gritty blue and olive-grey. For all our capacity to build places of tranquillity, it seems that we remain prone to conflict.

Initially the congregation would have comprised the landowner, for whom the Church was built and his tenants. To that extent we have moved on. As it's status grew, Wiggonholt had acquired burial rights by 1509 and now the parish around the wetlands was served also by neighbouring Greatham, Rackham, Parham and Amberley. As time moved on each era made its modest contribution to this spartan church. The plate is Elizabethan, the cup from 1675 and the wooden lid on the font dates from the Victorian era.

While it may not have been elevated to recognition by the poet laureate, it enjoyed recognition by at least an equal of Betjeman, amongst those critics of the post war brutalist style of architecture. In the early sixties Ian Nairn was a thorn in the side of the architects who knew better than we, what was good for us. His books on the disappearing characteristics of our town and landscape were best sellers and remain in print today. His timing was perfect and coincided with the emergence of a generation whose view of the world held certain aspects of the past in greater esteem than the mass produced and convenient of the modern world. Entry in one of his books (published by Penguin, no less), brought awareness to the much maligned 'masses'. In short, catching Ian Nairn's discerning eye speaks volumes for the virtue of the church. In Nairns' *The Buildings of England*, he describes Wiggonholt as 'small and sweet…down a tiny cul de sac'. His emergence down that lane revealed a single roomed church with a shingle bell turret and perpendicular windows. One books loss was another's gain, and if it is possible to immortalise a church, in literary terms, Nairn did so.

The last rays of winter sun caught the features of the three wise men, looking tired after their journey, in the nativity scene. They would shortly be returned to storage until next year, as part of a ritual that has been played out down the years.

That scene was placed upon the font, and I had always assumed such was created, to keep excited children quiet through the Christmas services. Only much later did it come to my attention that there has been a serious debate, bubbling away for decades, amongst astronomers who have produced a body of evidence that points towards the star actually rising in the sky, at about the time of the birth of Christ. The explanation, that the star was a miracle, drawing astronomers from a land east of Israel, was explanation enough for many. But following research of the American Museum - Hayden Planetarium's chairman, Dr Franklyn Branley, there is much evidence that the star of Bethlehem was a real phenomenon and the academic community now treat it as such.

Relying on historical and archaeological records, Branley believes that Jesus was actually born sometime between 8 B.C. and 4 B.C. If so, then the table of motions and positions of planets shows that there were three planets in the Autumn and Winter skies of 7 B.C. all of which moved closer together as the months went by. These planets were Mars, Jupiter and Saturn. By late Winter they had formed a small triangle. However, this couldn't easily be seen because the planets were low in the western sky. But, the Three Wise Men, were attributed with their title because of their knowledge of astronomy. They were given to gazing at the stars and the fact that the Bethlehem star below the horizon before full darkness came, is immaterial. At the risk of appearing flippant; a land bereft of television and street lights would create a people far more attuned to their surroundings and the night sky. The wise men would know about the positions and motions of planets, and that Jewish Rabbis claimed that the three planets were in constellation[2] centuries earlier, to mark the birth of Moses. As the three planets ultimately drew closer together, they formed the brightest light in the night sky. Thus, their conclusion that this was a sign, that an event of great importance was occurring, now appears to be the almost unavoidable conclusion for them to draw.

And that is why, some 2,000 years later there were Three Wise Men, looking on, in a model stable.

The Three Wise Men were perhaps the most modern, albeit temporary addition to the Church. It is delightfully unaltered and consequently, even homely albeit in an increasingly chilly way, as the doors opened for the few to slowly process out. The breeze straight off the Downs swiftly assailed us and an easy hub-hub of conversation broke out as we filed passed the font, *en route* to the porch.

It was my last chance to soak up the atmosphere and peer at my surroundings, until Candlemas in a months' time. Until then, the church would fall quiet, until the hushed arrival of passing wayfarers. They would pass under the porch, gently unhook the caged door intended to keep bird life out. The notices were evidence that this was still an active congregation; 'surely not, who comes here? But how quaint, oh look someone's made jam'. Hushed reverence; how is it that churches have such an impact upon us. Once the eyes adjust to the light, it all becomes clear.

All so peaceful, lest you comment on the font. Apparently, this is a matter of 'controversy'3. Some say it is Sussex marble, other say it is Purbeck stone.

Moving round the church the eye falls upon two scratch dials.4 These are on the south west corner and were used to indicate the time of services. Many of those that are left on churches around the country, date from Saxon times.

All in all, the erection of a church took wealth, from an era where food alone was far from plentiful. And I am troubled by the reference to the difficulties that rich men are presented with, upon endeavouring to enter the kingdom of heaven and in particular the comparative ease with which a camel may pass through the eye of a needle.5 It is as if my daily strivings, are misguided, should they ever be achieved.6 However, wealth and the Church, (both buildings and body) have historically been linked for so long. In the light of the camel's experiences, I would feel distinctly uneasy if anyone suggested that I should have a reserved seat in church. But Christianity came to Britain in an age where inequality was inevitable. The church, through its provision of education and justice,7 put us on the long hard road to progress. In getting there, we were dependent on our feudal masters for the provision of menial employment, tied cottages and a house of worship. It is perhaps futile to judge the past by the mores of the current era, for all generations stand on the shoulders the previous, who delivered us to where we are today, as they could, rather than perhaps as they should. Thus, it fell to the Bishop of Exeter to decide to whom to grant the Manor of Wiggonholt in 1444. From Syon, the manor moved to the 'Palmers of Angmering', all names quoted as if we should have some familiarity, as well we might centuries ago. After the dissolution of the Monasteries and a loosening of the manorial frame work, the links with nearby Angmering continued with the 'notable' family of the 'Penfolds' whose ancestors are believed to be the Pevenfauds whom appear on early taxation lists.

Up the lane that leads to the church is Wiggonholt Farm. The tenancy to the farm was assumed by Hugh Penfold in 1796, notwithstanding his own roots in Angmering. Hugh's baptism is probably that recorded in 1768 as 'son of John and Katren Penfold and it is he who is buried beneath the table tomb in the Churchyard and commemorated on a tablet in the Church along with the rest of his family. Indeed, the Penfolds have been laid to rest in Wiggonholt right up until 1895.

Life in the country can indeed be settled and slow, but population growth still presents its own problems[8]. And with it the occasional heinous crime. Let us take the case of local cobbler Thomas Carter from November 1489. Alas, had he kept to footwear he may have passed into tranquil anonymity, but no! Thomas had to turn his attention to 'brewing'. And with 'brewing' came trouble as he was reported for keeping '…an Inn of ill-repute and entertains sundry ill-conducted men and women for the public nuisance'. Life was hard and a fine should have kept him on the straight and narrow, as he'd failed to heed the warnings from the pulpit. By 1492 the hardships of a cobbler's life weakened his resolve and he fell foul of temptation once more and he was once again found '…receiving and lodging men and women, evilly disposed'. Life might have been so much better for Thomas Carter, had he succeeded in getting the job of work allocated to his namesake and fellow yeoman of Sussex, Thomas Blake for he was nothing less than 'Chief pledge taker and ale taster'[9].

The passage of time brings with it more regulations as perhaps it must. Thus it came to pass that a local byelaw was enacted that no tenant was allowed to let cattle graze the common fields or meadows without general consent, on pain of a fine. One such offender, was no less than the vicar! Discretion might dictate that we ignore an isolated transgression, but the Rev Guy Morley found his cattle's 'wanderlust' got the better of them on no fewer than 24 occasions. He is recorded as having 'put' his cattle into 'le west broke' attracting a fine of £4 or £1200 in today's money. But, members of the clergy were also the victims of crime. In 1607 one Cecily Payne broke into the parsonage and stole a smok and apron from the Rev Richard Bowley, for which she was sent to the gallows. It will be lost on few, that Cecily's plight fell short of complying with strict theological doctrine.

And even so, and even so, little could be said of the Wildbrook's history, that could detract from the feeling I have had, on each occasion, of complete peace. With that feeling we stepped out into the evening air. The elderly congregation bid their farewells as we took the path from the church door to the walled perimeter. There would be no stars tonight and spring seemed a long way away.

When I was subsequently writing these words I lifted my old copy of *The Kings England – Sussex* by Arthur Mee. In 1936 he had this to say about Wiggonholt:-

'*It is a beautiful place with it's gorse common and wide views; and it was an ancient place in Roman Days. A Roman villa has been discovered in a field on the Pulborough Road, and there are still mounds and terraced ways of those who lived in camps before the Romans came.*

The little one-roomed church, 13th and 15th century, has a big arcaded Norman font of Sussex marble, an Elizabethan cup, and two excellent sundials. A fragment of the old altar rails is preserved in the nave'.

What Sir John Betjeman appeared to have overlooked, other happened upon almost by accident. Now I am under no illusion that this book is hardly likely to sell in numbers that rectify our late poet lauriettes innocent oversight. But I do have to stress the draw of Wiggonholt. My intention had been to visit a different church each month over a period of 12 months. But as Candlemass approached precisely one month later in early February we found ourslves passing under it's modest yet welcoming arches once more.

Candlemass officially marks the end of Christmas, albeit that modern notions of 'dry January' and 'Veganuary' make it feel long gone. In fact it isn't, we've just spent up, which means I've historically missed the point along the way, but suspect I'm not alone.

And so we were met again by the lit candles aplenty, as the congregation welcomed each other, the lady at the door complimenting an elderly lady on sticks for having made it out for the first time since Christmas, passing out the hymn books[10], filing into the pews and eventually allowing the silence to return. Soon we settled down as if we'd been going for centuaries, as Steven once again gently roused the organ into life.

The congregation was even bigger than a month ago as we opened with:-

Blessed are you, Lord of Darkness, King of the universe,
You make our darkness to be light.
For with you is the well of life
And in your light shall we see light.
Blessed be God for ever.

One can attend Church through a number of life's seasons without *really* understanding; I did.

Now, according to long practised Jewish tradition, all new borns are inducted into Judaism by being presented to the temple shortly after birth. Jesus's birth was no different. And it was this which brought us together once more.

This and contemporary issues were included in the sermon. Life is always presenting its challenges, which whilst contemplated in an ancient building are as ever relavant; last month it was Iraq, this month we were just two days from having left the European Union. It heralded the end of three and a half years when the nation had been closer to civil war than for many a generation. It's scars will not be forgotten and few of us who lived through this period can claim to have approached the issue in a charitable and peaceful way inkeeping with the many sermons that had touched on the issue. The Vicar was mindful of this event but equally ready to point out that there was another issue looming that would dominate her forthcoming sermons; she was about to become a Grandmother!

As we were leaving I caught sight of a very old lady at the back of the church. She was almost in the phoetal position and her gaze was resting on the light from the candle which she was holding. Grey whisps of hair poked out from under her woolen hat and when occasional parishoners went over to her she scarcely looked up, but smiled briefly utterly content with herself in that moment. My imagination ran away with itself, as I discreetly observed her alongside the font and wondered if her life had perhaps started there many years earlier.

We made our way up the path where the crocusses were now poking through the ground where there had been no sign of spring a month ago. The lane which the Romans, Arthur Mee, Cecily Blake and Thomas Carter knew so well, took us to the A272 and our own age. We had been slow to leave Wiggonholt and swift to return. I suspect it shall remain that way.

1. I confess to being carried away here. I cannot confirm if the trees were indeed elm, and am sure that the organist wasn't a school mistress on account of being called Steven. But it sums up the 'flavour' of the church that evening.
2. Constellation – quite literally, *'any of the groups of stars in the sky that seem from earth to form a pattern and have been given names',*
3. An indication, perhaps of the lack of troubles locally, that it is nothing more serious than the source of stone that is a matter of controversy – or a tongue in cheek comment in the guide book?
4. Also known as Mass Dials, these were a very early and primitive form of sun dial. They were used by priests to advertise the time of the next service. Usually in the form of a semi-circle about ten inches across, they were scratched into the south wall of the church. A hole was bored at the centre and a number of lines scratched from the hole to the arc. The priest would place a short stick in the hole and when the sun shone the shadow of the stick on to one of the lines, the next service would start.
5. 'It is easier for a camel to pass through the eye of a needle, then for a rich man to enter the kingdom of heaven'. Matthew 19:24.
6. However, I do not doubt that the full theological explanation would enlighten.
7. Subsequently taken over by the state, to varying degrees of satisfaction.
8. Perhaps not spectacular, but a factor – 1641, 30 men over 18, 1724, 7 families, 1801, 42 and 1851, 39. And not one social worker!
9. Thomas Blakes full title was 'Chief pledge and ale taster for the tithing' and also a 'beadle'. As such he was a minor parish official who acted as usher and kept order. But it is perhaps his role as 'ale taster' that was the more attractive. All such gossip has been faithfully recorded for posterity in the court rolls for various local manors.

10. Mine happened to be marked 'Easter 1947'.

Chapter Two

St Mary's, Slaugham.

'Do come in – visitor light switch is on the left'.

Any church with such a notice in the porch, must be worth a visit. No sooner had I stepped inside the bright and airy Norman church than I was met with another sign on a pillar, proclaiming 'He is risen'.

In the silence I felt curiously welcome, despite being entirely alone. It was the first Saturday afternoon of lent.

The previous week, I had read in the 1958 edition of the *Collins Guide To English Parish Churches* that the entries were on the basis of whether or not they were worth cycling twelve miles in the rain to visit. Alas, the start of this calender year was a pockmark of named storms – Atiyah, Brendan, Ellen,

Francis, Gerda and, would you believe, Iris. I've never been particularly scared of an Iris before, but this year it would be different. And so I set out, pedalling frantically against the tail end of storm Ciara, trembling in anticipation at the arrival of storm Dennis, comfortable in the knowledge that I was setting a higher bar for entry into my modest tombe, than that set by our erstwhile poet lauriette. For all that, we are both agreed that St Mary's at Slaugham deserves an entry, to which the guide reads briefly:-

'Slaugham (St Mary) Mostly 14th cent.; 16th cent. Brasses'

Luckily I hadn't read the entry before I started pedalling, otherwise I might not have bothered. And thankfully it became quickly clear that there's much more to St Mary's, Slaugham, than 'brasses'.

You might come across Slaugham by accident, on your way to 'somewhere'. Slaugham just seems in between elsewhere, on a section of rasied ground, in a forest, yet close to Crawley, Horsham and Haywards Heath. One suspects this tiny affluent connurbation has more stock brokers than foresters these days. And then it's gone in a flash, yet I wondered how many weary heads had paused, parked up in the car park in front of the church and stepped inside, momentarily away from the worries of the world. For Slaugham is singularly inviting.

Amongst the hush of the trees that surround it, I suspect that many have sat in the silence and wondered, if there's another way. And there I sat, noting that a church errected in an austere era, steeped in tradition is very much in the 21st century. The south aisle has a separate section, tidily piled with toys and child sized chairs. Yet facing them on the north aisle, a plaque draped in the union flag – with the names of the fallen in two world wars. Alan, Norman, John and sixty five more. Perhaps the laughter of children rebounds off the stone into which their names are chizelled, when sunday school is in full swing.

If it is true that every village is interesting which has an ancient church – then we may be right to conclude that the current church itself is the most authentic record of the history of the village'.

A quote I shamelessley lifted from the visitor guide, but so true.

And I suspect the current parishoners will go down in this particular chapter of their history as a gentle body of people. For 'Progress' can be brutal as the comparison between the old Coventry Cathedral and the new demonstrates, to some at least. [11] But the mild mannered parishoners have contributed to progress too – now brace yourself ; they've changed the pews for comfortable seats. Gone are those dark hardwood pews with backs at ninety degrees, designed to keep farm hands and foresters, capable of wandering thoughts, wide awake during the sermon.

Alas, Churches haven't always been known for their comfort and welcome; pews at the front for the squire despite our equality in the eyes of the Lord, children to be seen and not heard and all that. And woe betide anyone who turned up in sandals brandishing a tambourine. But in Slaugham there 'feels' like they've had a gentle evolution and have got it just right.

The 'ham' of Slaugham means 'home'and the Church[12] proabbly dates back to the Norman period. Those comfy seats are not the first evolutionary step in St Mary's long history, or the most radical. Had a visitor been passing in 1613 they might have indignantly penned in the visitors book of the day '…pray, who on earth agreed to build the Covert Chapel'. They could have continued '…or completely fill in the the round headed doorway, or replace the chancel with a nave[13], or repalce the organ chamber with a combined vestry. And who dared to move the mural tablets to the north wall to allow the insertion of an arch'. The changes continued through the 1970s and on, which when you consider the architectural delights the 70s have left us with, shows that the people of Slaugham knew how to resist the fashionable ill considered onslaught of the day.[14]

For the sentimental (me)[15] the church is the place that you always come back to. The place that is brought into sharpest focus on your return from college for your first Christmas holiday. The one place where there is no discernable change, of familiar faces and a pattern to life that stimulates the question, is 'elsewhere' really an improvement? And in some parishes a place where overbearing parents parade their offspring replete with newly acquired college scarves, which stimulate observations from the author, that have no place in any book with even the faintest trace of a theologocal inclination. Alas, by the New Year it was nice to have been, but the forthcoming term is invading one's thoughts as the bags are packed. Easter looms, while in the bright cold mornings, the redoubtable mothers of the parish will gather to quietly arrange the flowers, privately wondering what their offspring got up to the night before (and are they eating properly?).

In distant halls of residence, a brief thought is spared for the mothers. An anchor in a world presenting challenges, such challenges being faced, safe in the knowledge that when it becomes too much, the old world will provide its refuge.

Only a little changes, bit by bit. All to soon the bands of marriage are read out and life, and the Church moves on. A return with grandchildren to a church now occupied by other families. In a pew on which I once sat, they recite the Lord's Prayer from the inscription on the wall, as I could do from the back of the Church. Now I would need a pair of binnoculars – or so I chose to confide to the new Vicar.

Ah let me enter once again the pew
Where the child nodded as the sermon
grew
Scene of soft slumbers! I remember now
The chiding finger, and the frowning brow

The 'new people', as we once were, turn and ask, 'have been in the village long?', to which my late father could only answer in all honesty, 'since 1967'.
For I am now, briefly one of the 'new people' to Slaugham, and in 'my church' hundreds of miles away, sits my couterpart. Possibly.

And in this gentle setting I sat in solitude, to take in the moment. A building whose airy silence is only occasionally interupted by the stirring of the trees outside – I wondered what intrinsic value a building has that enables it to exude peace, just by being. Is it it's age, location, design or the feeling of following a path trod over a millenia? This is a big question, but rest assured, in sitting in St Mary's, one is just happy to be.

Be that as it may, Churches were not built by reflective blokes on bicycles dropping in on a wet Saturday afternoon. They may exude peace now, but the Parishoners of old had to be driven, as was noted in *Parish Churches of England*16*:-*

'Apart from the spiritual aspects of the case, the pride and pleasure of medieval people in their chruches was very real, and the local patriotism that, in the bad state of communications, enhanced the rivalries between town and town, parish and parish, often found its proudest expression in the church building. With the exception of the castles, which always absorbed a percentage of the labour, the majority of the funds and skill available was concentrated on the raising of the churches.'

Whatever the motivation, the Church has been in a continual state of respectful evolution since mediavel times – with the exception of the curious construction of a public house, right in front of the Church - The White Horse Inn, which came and went, leaving not a trace. This 'pub' post dated many of the first alterations as the oldest part of the church that remains is the round headed Norman doorway – now filled in. The south aisle was added in the thirteenth century, along with the chancel – clearly it was a very modest church at the ouset, as to an amatuer like I, the absence of the foregoing leaves very little to constitute a church (in architectural terms, at least).

Leap forward to 1858 and the west wall of the covert chapel was removed to facilitate the enlargement of the South Aisle , organ chamber and combined vestry. The upper upper part of the tower was also rebuilt, retaining its Sussex cap. On into the 20th century and by 1921 the chancel needed restoration whereon to the memory of one Charles Pickard Warren, oak choir stalls, side screens, altar rails rerodos and two figures on the east wall, one either side of the altar, were added.

And down the ages the same challenges face each parish, for there amongst all the paraphernalia of the Parish, lay a leaflet for the Handcross Community Pantry – 'Free

Provisions For The Local Community'. Every Saturday 10am till 12pm at all Saints Church Handcross. In normal times, at least.

I paused and picked up the St Mary's Slaugham Parish News for January/February 2020. As I fully expected it was full of the quaint every day details of village life, a note from the Handcross Ladies Association, details of the Community Bus service, adverts for the services of a lady rat catcher, landscaper, garden fencer and funeral director. All sandwiched between an article titled 'Home For Christmas' on the migrating Black cap warbler and another on earthworms (was there a connection?). When Londoners, who are but half an hour to the north, contemplate a move to the country, it is this image of Village life that draws them out. But, unknown to the Rector, who penned the opening words, with an article headed simply 'Help', the forthcoming year would lay bare the virtue of thinking of others – not least in case we need them to think of us. In the words of the said Rector:-

'Whats the bravest thing you ever said?'
'Help'

Rural communities are not immune from the Facebook age of putting on a front, to show one's perfect existance to the world. He went on:-

'The reality is that whatever you are struggling with, you are not alone...This is at the Heart of all we are seeking to be a church community. This is at the heart of the Handcross Community Pantry, the toddler groups, the soup lunches, the parenting courses and hopefully one day our Sunday mornings – creating places where we can come as we are...'

As I sat there in the silence, it was hard to imagine that the sinews that held communities together, were about to be tested as hardly ever before. That asking for and giving help, might be essential to ensure our future existance.

11. Shame on me, I haven't visited either the old or the new Coventry Cathedral. And I feel that those town planners who overlooked the ruins of their ancient town, following five years of war, can't be blamed for wanting to completely break from the past. It was all around them and in ruins. Yet the returning heroes expetcted a New Jerusalem. But the comparison is brutal – and people are now supremely sensitive to change, but they did it gently in little old Slaugham. We'd do well to learn.

12. Or another church on the same site.

13. Which took place as early as the 13th century.

14. All in all, the chairs may have caused comment in the visitor book, but clearly far more radical changes have been happening within this delightful church, more or less continuously over its long life. Indeed in the 1970 a glazed oak screen was errected as '...a token of the deep gratitude for many blessings received by members of the Paterson, Folke and Whyte families 1970'.

15. Quite shamelessly. Add to that amateur and deeply suspicious of 'experts' – self appointed or otherwise.

16. By J. Charles Cox LL.D. F.S.A. A Batsford Book 1943-1944.

Chapter Three

St Marks, Staplefield.

The year began with me being determined to write a book titled *Evensong In Susssex* – but by the time I visited Staplefield, it was becoming obvious that my first choice for the title might be inappropriate. Even so, I opened the first draft of this chapter – 'Forgive me, for this book is about evensong. And evensong in Sussex. And whilst we are in Sussex, this is the second church I have taken you to, where the visit did not coincide with evensong.'Perhaps 2021 will be altogether different. Yet I concluded as we pedalled towards St Marks that the opportunity to pay a visit 'was just too good to miss'.

As with so many churches worth a visit, it is one that you might find yourself just passing by. For the United Benefice of St

Mary's & St Marks encompassing Staplefield common is on the old London to Brighton road, long bypassed by the roaring M23. It's on a straight section passed the oft used cricked ground, overlooked by two public houses. But on this day in early March, the Club house was closed, the nets blew in the wind and the sightscreens lay forlornly on their sides. All such a long way from balmy summer evenings of India Pale Ale and ripple of applause.

'Flowing together by devious chanels
From farm and brickyard, forest and
dene, Thirteen men in glittering flannels
Move to their stations out on the green'[15]

And then it's gone in a flash as the promise of Brighton beckons. But my son and I had put Staplefield to the *cycle in the rain* test, one Sunday afternoon in early March. The skies were heavy and leaden and the wind blustery as we set out against it. Through St Leonards Forest, up and down and around the hammer ponds; were we really underneath the flight path to an international airport? It didn't feel like it today.

But the cricket field was empty, and the Morris Dancers of summer a distant memory. Not even a sullen teenager on their phone in a bus shelter, as is their collective wont. All was quiet but windy.

There is a map by a lane which, due to my inability to read it correctly, sent me up the wrong road to look for the Church. Eventually we found it at the centre of the village alongside the school. As with most parish churches, they are to be found alongside seats of learning as historically, only the church had the capacity, or inclination to educate the 'common folk'.

We made our way up the sweeping path to the church entrance, overlooked by the Spanish style bell tower.[16]

The church porch is invariably the introduction to the soul of the community, it's activites, the forthcoming coffee morning, a call for volunteers to cut the grass, donate to the food bank and a reminder, that we are in the season of Lent.

Flicking through the chanels of the televsion on a Sunday evening, one might happen upon *Songs of Praise* and come across references to Lent and conclude that it is possibly just another incomprehensible Christian ritual [17]. It is a period of reflection (in a less than reflective age), in which Christians prepare themselves for the crucifiction and resurrection of Jesus. During these forty days Christians replicate Jesus's forty days in the wilderness by fasting and abstinance.[18] It is also for prayer and pennance. And with that in mind I gently heaved open the mighty creaking door.

Staplefield on this partcular afternoon was dim and silent. There was no complimentary lighting and the air hung with that musty smell, familiar of all old churches. The arrival in a Church arouses a sense of peace, permanence and security. A reminder of a childhood reluctantly spent on hard pews, where life was certain and such uncertainties as arose, were rapidly dispensed with by dependable parents.

In this particular year, some worried about Brexit as if it was a portend for the end of civilization. Others about President Trump, as if his single foray into the Middle East heralded the onset of Armageddon.

I had set out to write this book with a reflective entry from each parish, each month. Yet each month brought new headlines that at the time of writing seemed destined to dominate the year; but hadn't. Therefore it was, as we entered the month of March, of only minor concern that in far away China, a virus had spread that was predicted to wreak havoc across the globe. In the last four or five years the doom mongers had stated that havoc

was coming for various unrelated reasons, and yet it never arrived
. One could almost sense their disappointment. We were, as a nation, quite tired of worrying over things that might never happen. It was therefore with a slight sense of detatchment that we watched the scenes from Wuhan in China. That was China, and this was Staplefield and my son had just ascended the pulpitt to discover that someone had left the microphone on.

As with all churches, St Marks had its parish history chizelled into it's walls and ultimately laid to rest in the grave yard.

Ofcourse it had a feeling of permanace as all old churches have, except St Marks is not by Sussex standards a particularly old church.

It seemed that it had been built just long enough for lichen to have grown about it's stonework and on the gravestones, but that aside the church dates back to no earlier than 1846, when its first collection was received. And with that, the building works began.

At first the information that follows is dry but slowly becomes alarming. We have a parish of '330 persons'[19]. Yet they have built a mini continental cathedral with high ceilings into which their praise is consumed. The site, which cost the princely sum of £40 to purchase lies 241ft and 6 inches above sea level. The entire cost was £2,522. The Rev T.A. Maberley donated the silver altar vessels for the Holy Communion and Mrs Maberley donated the stone font. And the consecration was finally undertaken by the Bishop of Chichester on the 18th of November 1847. And what is alarming is how such a small parish, with such a modest sized congregation had managed to errect such a magnificent church in the heart of the English countryside.

As I strolled up the nave, I was struck by the spartan nature of the Church. There was very little that was ornamental; continental it may have felt, Catholic it was not. And then I found myself in the Chancel. Briefly the sunlight made it's presence felt through the east window and onto the altar. And there just below the ceiling and above the alter, various murals reminiscent of the Arts & Craft's movement (they lived around here too).

It transpires that the murals were the work of one Charles Eamer Kempe, whose work also adourns cathedrals as grand as Chester, Gloucester, Hereford, Lichfield, Wells, Winchester and York. And little old Staplefield. For why? Well, Kempe is a 'local lad' hailing from down that said road in nearby Brighton. [20] It was whilst at Oxford, that he witnessed William Morris design the debating chamber at the famous Oxford

Union. The experience was one of two significant factors that lead Kemp away from the ministry. The other was his severe speech impediment which lead him to conclude:-

"if I was not permitted to minister in the Sanctuary, I would use my talents to adorn it"

And thus, the Ministry's loss was the churches gain. On page 38 his painted trees can be seen on the patterned walls. The roof timbers have also been painted to illustrate psalm 117:-

Praise the LORD, all you nations; extol him, all you peoples. For great is his love toward us, and the faithfulness of the LORD endures forever. Praise the LORD.

A failure to understand the virtues of the past is not a modern phenomenon. When appreciating the recently passed, it is 'old hat', whereas appreciating the long gone it is renaissance. But where is the cross over? That dilemma faced earlier generations when they decided to paint over the lower parts of the nave thereby hiding for eternity some of Kemp's stencilling. Incredible to even contemplate now, but perhaps not so difficult then.

Thankfully greater consideration came in to play when restoring the well. It was decided in 2009 that the line had long been crossed and there was a greater appreciation of Kemp and his contemporaries. Upon removing the grime, they discovered his delicate colour scheme and a signature of his accomplice A E Tombleson. Happily, it was all allowed to stay.

On so many occasions, setting concrete is signed, adorned with hand prints or has buried bottles with a message, as in our own small way we seek posterity. Perhaps the craftsman momentarily contemplates the prospect of ever being rediscovered, and what will the age look like when that occurs?

The murals intrigued me, but there was more; much more to St Marks. Is this unique church really set in the county of which it was once said:-

'The churches of Sussex are many and various. They are not among the most magnificent since, unlike East Anglia and Gloucestershire, there was no flourishing local industry here when Gothic architecture reached it's Zenith in the 15th century…(and few religious foundations with Churches)…survived the Dissolution…' 21.

I do not for a minute set out to assert that I, or this book has any right to challenge conventional thinking. I am a shameless amateur. And the church was built for all. But I hope to convey the 'feeling' of a church and I was finding that, notwithstanding the apparent lack of *magnificence*, the churches of Sussex, were far from left wanting.

In addition to his murals, Kemps talents extended to stained glass. In 1868 the south chancel side windows were fitted with windows, featuring single figures. These were reminiscent of Morris & Co and made by the famous T Ballie & Sons to whom Kemp trusted most of his early work.

The detail of St Marks continues to impress as through the ages (1868 – 1924), the church was adorned with a succession of new stained-glass windows, not least when Kemp & Co replaced a Pugin[22] stained glass window.

Kemps talents also graced the church one last time in 1880 when he added that triple belfry, that caught my eye at the outset, to the Ferrey's tower.

All in all, Staplefield, like all churches has that feel of permanence, in a throw away age. That alone is testament to its virtue; so well constructed were they, that neither the weather or the passage of time could erode their dominance in any village. That, alas, is a myth, for there is a harsh reality to maintaining these old buildings; one lost amidst the organ recitals, murals and the peel of bells that disturbs the doves from the roof tops. Unseen and taken for granted, there lies a grumbling source of trouble, for in Staplefield they've had a lot of trouble with the boiler over the years! It kept the evacuated children of St James the Less, Westminster who arrived here in 1939, perfectly warm for the duration of their stay. The troops who arrived in 1941 had their own services in the Church and still it's heat coursed through the pipes. Bells, organ and the clock had money lavished on them, but by 1951 it was necessary to spend the princely sum of £75-15-6 on the unseen unattractive lump.

One can almost picture the Parochial Church Council consuming modest quantities of cheese and wine in the vicarage, whilst discussing the great events of the parish; the publication of the History of Staplefield[23], the rededication of the five bells[24], the donation of the painting of the Madonna and Child by Oliver Messel[25], and the arrival of the new neighbours for morning prayer, HRH Princess Margaret[26] and celebrity photographer Lord Snowdon[27]. Then, as the last olive was being mercilessly pursued around an ill poised plate by a cocktail stick, the groundsman has to interject 'but what about the boiler?'

Elsewhere, 1966 might go down in history for many reasons, but at St Marks, they finally took delivery of their new oil fired church boiler[28]. A great event indeed.

And it was to the outside, in the calming wind of early spring, that I returned to look again at the distinctive bell tower. It was reminiscent of Greece, or Spain, a tower that might protrude from a sun-baked hill side. Like everything else, they came at a cost and in 1968 they had to be rehung at the sum of £395-1-0.

My thoughts turned once again to my imaginary groundsmen and his practical interjection into the polite conversation of the ladies of the parish, at the vicarage tea party. As efforts were made to impress the super posh new neighbours, the Ladies gently sipping Darjeeling from their used *once in a while* china, look upon his hoary hands gripping a cucumber sandwich and hold their breath, should he regale HRH with the extortionate cost of facilitating a peel of bells on the sabbath. A practical man, he's there because he's hungry, they are there for an entirely different reason, perhaps not entirely devotional.

The enduring quality of the parish church is its reassuring feel of unwavering permanence in a changing age. Yet in many ways three worlds met at the vicarage tea party. For my Ladies with their china cups:-

Phone for the fish knives, Norman
As cook is a little unnerved;
You Kiddies have crumpled the serviettes
And I must have these things daintily served[29]

Of course, with a Royal in their midst, they would not believe all these stories of wild parties with gangsters and pop stars. But the princess had married a London Dandy whom I picture sporting a velvet jacket and flares, allowing his wife to make small talk with beaming ladies who would live off the encounter for years to come. Perhaps he just couldn't wait to leave and return to more familiar territory: -

...among climbing plants, lumps of driftwood,
and heaps of pebbles, pairs of velvet trousers
were displayed on dummies that finished
abruptly just above the waist; faceless busts
in what looked a bit like bronze wore shorts of
ribbed corduroy, flashed gigantic wrist
watches, had their necks encircled by flowing

scarves evidently made out of somebody's aunties summer dress. 30

And there, having been manoeuvred to the fringes, our groundsman looks incomprehensibly (and perhaps a little hungrily) upon the scene. He's never been to London and doesn't want to. And neither will he ever understand why he always ends up almost out of sight at events like this, but at the forefront when it comes to tidying up when everyone has left. Some things never change.

15.Village Green by Gerald Bullett (1893-1958).

16.Or was it Greek, or ancient Byzantine? I know not for sure.

17. Matthew 4:1

18. This year I had given up alchohol, whereas a friend of my son, sincerely committed to giving up broccoli. Still it could have been worse, when I was at school I remember someone asserting sincerely that they were giving up Church.

19. '...of which 300 sittings must be kept free and unappropriated forever'. Egalitarian it may sound, it also reveals that there were 30 toffs around about.

20. He is the cousin of Thomas Reade Kemp, a politician and property developer who is responsible for the devlopment of Brighton's Kemptown district.

21. Collins Guide to English Parish Churches.

22. Ah Pugin; lawyers despair. Well into the millenium Pugin became byword for ostentatious living, when one Lord Chancellor, cut back on Leagal Aid (for the people) whilst spending over £50,000 on Pugin wall paper (for himself) with public money. Such a reaction, 150 years or so since Pugin's death is an indication of his standing. And Kemps, to have eclipsed him, in Staplefild at least.

23. By the Rev W A Dengate (1947)

24. By the Rt Rev H M Horden (1948)

25 Donated by Mrs Messel (1958)

26 6th October 1961 whereon the local Mothers Union presented the Princess with a layette for her new born son.

27 As he was to become, up until then he was Tony Arsmtrong Jones a resident of Handcross and known for his conviviality (not least to the authors one time land lady). It's a small community.

28. As well it might be at £496-9-0.

Chapter Four

The Lonely Church in the Forest.

A crimson cloud bank was massing to the west. At the start of our cycle ride, my son and I could kidd ourselves that we would escape the rain, but now it seemed unlikely. We were hungry and had just pulled some food from or panniers, and sat eating as the first rain drops fell.

The second Sunday of the month is significant, for that is when evensong is celebrated at St John the Evangelist, Coolhurst. And this trip was a preamble to that visit, planned for the second Sunday in March 2020, a sigificant date of which I was then blissfully unaware.

St Johns is set in an isolated location in a forest. Deer and pheasants seemed to be the main company as we ate our fruit. In each setting, it has been difficult to believe that on the same planet where we are surrounded by peace and tranquility, there are those whose lives are imperilled. The Holy Lands today are far from happy and they have dominated sermons in these very churches, for nearly two decades now. And those we elect have set in motion the events that have lead to such unhappiness for the same period. The war in Syria was reaching a climax, and refugees were massing at the border. Western governments (particularly ours) were wedded to simple solutions for complex problems. I predicted with some confidence that this would be the dominant theme of the month ahead. I too was completely wrong.

And still the cock pheasant picked its way through the undergrowth.

At first it happened gradually. At work our AGM was cancelled because of news headlines over 5,000 miles away; the coronavirus was coming, but then again so was Brexit. Like all headlines, they had an unreal feel to them and we live in an age when out collective view of the media is at an all time low. Thus a colleague relieved of the AGM, decided instead to go to London for a wild night out. Another colleague suggested we could still attend our networking event at the local cricket club. But there were murmurings about gatherings of 25 or more. He was phlegmatic until further guidance came from our management team. As I emailed my declination to the cricket club, I felt slightly embarrassed at being so cautious. I got a cheerful reply, hoping to see me at the next one. I too looked forward to it. Clearly we had overreacted.

And then the cricket club cancelled. I took my son to his last cricket practice, and attended church where the Vicar advised that coffee after church was cancelled. And instead of sharing the peace, we would wish our fellow worshippers by sign language, careful not to announce two very similar signs which indicate either 'twins' or 'baking'. And then rather than have coffee we mingled in a different part of the church and thus introduced ourselves to different members of the congregation whom we found ourselves alongside. Quizically we looked at each other, 'what's all this about then?' Little did we know that this would be our last church service for some time.

And the sun shone. Our son phoned from the park where he had gone to with the choir, 'adults are having picnics just like normal, can I go on the outdoor gym?'

'Why do you think they have closed the indoor gym?'

It all seemd so very normal, except for the lack of coffee.

The following day, there were meetings; it'll all be over in a fortnight.

And still the sun shone. We will all be encouraged to work at least two days a week from home. I will get fit – each morning my son and I cycled for miles. Then the office will be closed for 21 days. I will get really fit. Was I the only one who at the outset looked forward to this change from the mundane routine?

Then the pubs closed, as did the restaurants. The last mass gathering seemed to be the Bath marathon, where we had visited weeks before without a thought.

The front page of one national newspaper had a picture of a lady, replete with face mask, praying at a church in China. And China is better known for pulling churches down; could they be having second thoughts?

Every capital in the World emptied. Completely. We had never seen anything like it before.

And then people started dying. Britain built a massive 5,000 bed hospital in nine days flat. The NHS, already close to the hearts of all Britons, moved considerably closer to the epicentre of our souls.

Panic buying ceased, rationing by social censure brought us closer to the realization of our new normal. On a lighter note the effect had left us with a new turn of phrase coined reliably by a British tabloid; 'The Bog Roll Bandit', applied to those who stockpiled lavatory paper…for some reason.

Another headline had a picture of a man in London holding up a sign which read 'Jesus is coming soon'. In another age he would be dismissed as a crank. Somehow it didn't seem so out of place.

The flight path under which we live hosts over 900 flights a day. As I write these words I have heard one today. The filthy waters of Venice[31] cleared with alarming speed and are now a home to fish, rather than tourists. On the fringes some people called it a wake up call. Beyond the fringes, even more wondered if they might have a point, even if it didn't do to concur in polite company.

With the absence of traffic came bird song, whilst the NHS worked around the clock, all too many making the ultimate sacrifice for people they had never even met.

And it all happened so quickly. By 6.15pm on the evening of Sunday the 5th of

April 2020 another 621 people had died in Britain, bringing the total to 4,394. Both the Health Secretary and the Prime Minister had caught the virus, the former losing two loved ones.

That morning we had opened the French windows and sat down to watch our local Church service on line. It was Palm Sunday. The reader was sat in her home, the sermon from the clergy in the vicarage, the congregation all sat in their respective homes apart, but somehow together. A recording of the hymns from earlier services brought back recent memories of the normal, that we had taken for granted. The faces in the congregation of those we know, nod to or who are complete strangers came flooding back. It was an unusal but not unpleasant experience.

And I think back to that everyday event of a father and son going for a cycle ride. I do not really know when we will go back to the lonely church in the forest. It should have been a fortnight ago now.

To add to the authenticity of my account of these trips I asked my son if he remembered our ride to the lonely church. He confirmed he did.

'What did you think of it?'

'It was just like all the others'.

Thank God for our children.

And so he plays badminton with his Mum in our back garden, as the sun sets in a planeless sky, illuminating the skeletal out line of trees only just hosting the first signs of spring.

It all looked so normal but was so different. We had been asked, in that uniquely British way (as oppose to told), not to pass through our own front doors. Our families might be couped up for three months for no instantly comprehensible reason. And the vast majority of people did that without a murmur.

When it came to good deeds, people scarcely needed to ask. We had seemed to find some long dormant gene, subdued in an age of selfish isolation, that suddenly knew what to do, as if the war[32] had ended only the day before. The stories came in of good deeds, a nation pulling together – the stuff of folk lore; but this time it really happened.

And then a call did finally go out for volunteers to assist the NHS, perhaps in the hope that they might find an extra 50,000 helpers or 100,000 at a push. This very weekend the number had exceeded 500,000 with the new target being extended to 750,000.

The Queen broadcast to the nation at 8pm that evening and said:-

"I hope in the years to come everyone will be able to take pride in how they responded to this challenge. And those who come after us will say the Britons of this generation were as strong as any"

Praise indeed from one who has seen so much.

31. A city with fewer waterways than Birmingham. But will we forget that when the virus is over?
32. The war; why is it always the war? Alas, I recall those who lived through it saying how supportive people were as a nation, until the day the war ended and everyone went back to being there usual selfish selves. It spoils a good story, but it did come from those who know.

Chapter Five

St Nicholas, Itchingfield.

…provided a glimpse of paradise lost. A heavenly silence on a spring day, reached through a kaleidoscope of differing tones of green, bordering a road lined with motherwort and hedgerow. A steep hill lead into clear blue sky punctuated by the occasional cloud, interrupted only by the mewing of distant circling buzzards.

Were we really under a flight path, twenty miles from the M25? It seemed unlikely, but as we reached the top of the hill and looked back, we could see the same Sussex as the novice parson might once have stopped to take in, as he made his way to his new Parish of St Nicholas, Itchingfield. Long before the tilting fingerpost road sign gave a clue to his whereabouts, he might have stopped to take a breath and wonder what his latest mission had in store for him in this parish perched on a ridge, disturbed only by a gentle breeze.

We were five weeks into the lockdown and we had never seen anything like it before. It would be easy to say that in this nation, famous for well mannered queues, that the populations acceptance of the restrictions had been remarkable. But so had everywhere else around the globe, without exception.

And so we freewheeled along the top of the ridge to St Nichloas's Church. We were entierly alone save for a gardener kneeling by his flower bed.

The lockdown continued to present many challenges and much heartache. But it would be easy to conclude, were it not for the news, that the nation had simply reversed a century and people were reconnecting with simpler values.

We freewheeled on and somewhere in the distant summer haze drifted the sound of a ringing bell. Indeed for the first time in over a decade, this bell could be heard across our town, as the bypass that divided the town from the bell tower had fallen silent. Like the sound of shire horses pulling the plough, it came from an age long before my birth, yet strangely upon hearing either for the first time it put me at ease, as if it portended my arrival at an old familiar home – clearly it couldn't really be anything of the sort.

And so we walked the flagstone path into Itchingfield Churchyard. The grass grew tall and a chorus of grasshoppers greeted us. The Church was closed but alive with life.

Every September the Sussex Historic Churches Trust runs a sponsored 'Ride 'n' Stride' in which cyclists and walkers travel between parishes to find a quiet welcome from a member of the congregation, who invariably parts from pollishing the brasses to pass a drink and the time of day. We sign the book and note that insanely fit member of our congregation has beaten us to it and will clock up many more before the day is done. But within those pages is the name of someone who has cycled up from Worthing and one can sense a growing urgency from their respective signatures that there just might be a hint of rivalry emerging. But all that was before 'the lockdown'. On this day, the sun shone and our tired legs (for we had just climbed the hill), carried us down the flagstone path.

When Hollywood directors go in search of a quintessentially English Church, the image in their minds eye of what they are looking for, is probably very similar to Itchingfield.

And so we made our way along the path towards the Porch.

Resolutely locked.

All so different from the sunny days of the 'Ride 'n' Stride'. Then the sultry heat beat down, the sun being interrupted by a dark cloud as a cool draft arose from nowhere. Soon there was a downpour and we duly dashed into the porch. Shortly, the cloud passed and the church yard became alive with bird song and insect life, all in sufficient time to recover from the ride. Now we could take in our surroundings, under the shade of the yew, whilst stopping for lunch. We were entirely alone amongst the grave stones and pied wagtails that rapidly grew used to our presence.

To the right, the Curate's cottage[33], apparently empty. The wattle and daub has withstood the test of time and there are some that would be happy to live there now. I pondered the prospect of climbing the worn oak stairs, each night knowing that young curates had done the same for centuries. Their worries might be limited to wondering if the local landowners had paid their tythe to ensure his existance. Well, if you must have worries, here's as peaceful a place to have them as any.

Beautiful as the day was, it fell short of the days of the Ride 'n' Stride when tea and buscuits awaited those who'd made the climb. Then as now the sun beat down but it was high summer and the interior of the church provided a very welcome relief from the burning heat. Then we sat aching but content in the 12th century building as the daylight brought the stained glass window to life. For those who've taken a pew, there rises behind them a 15th century wooden tower. A ride throught the Sussex countryside will reveal these towers in nearby Newdigate and Burstow – in fact I don't recall ever seeing them until I came to Sussex. The tower is constructed around four posts and heavily braced and boarded on the outside. Elsewhere in the church is to be found a Table of Kindred Affinity proclaiming 'Wherein Whosoever Are Related Are Forbidden by the Church of England to Marry Together', just to put the matter beyond doubt. Elsewhere a beautifully polished brass plaque to the memory of the fallen of 1914-1918 reflects the colours of the window depicting Jesus on the cross.

Outside the occasional cyclist wheeled their cycles down the flagstone path. The tranquility encourages reverance as they gently make their way to the refeshments to sign the visitors book, their cycling shoes clicking on the stone floor. And reverential they might well be, for whilst this church is no exception to the rule that many get sympathetically developed and maintained over the centuries, much remains from the year 1125 including two walls and a window, and a recess (known as an aumbry) in the church wall. In an earlier restoration his Reverance even took it upon himself to to carve his initials in 1713! Later, one Sir Gilbert Scott directed a significant restoration in the 19th century and discovered a Norman alter which is in use today.

But in the year of coronavirus, all of the foregoing was behind the locked door. Then as now, it was a beautiful day and quite understandable why the conreagation should proudly proclaim:-

We are surrounded by our lovely churchyard which provides a rich and varied habitat for the local flora and fauna and a peaceful, reflective space for visitors. It's a real jewel of God's creation.

And so it is. But the time had come for us to slowly move from where we were slumped under a tree. A last look at the 16th Century Priest House stimulates the query if we might all be happier if we lived like the paid cleric for whom it was built, rather than working to consume and ultimately throw away in an ever decreasing time scale. Eighty years after the construction another cottage was built, and the Priest house became an Almshouse along with a dedicated garden[33] in which the residents grew produce – clearly the lack of a local Waitrose did not encumber their existance. For cooking they were able to gather firewood from the local woodland as well as rabbits and birds to eat. Clearly they thought of everything, but life moves on and the creation of the Union Workhouse in nearby Horsham caused it to fall into disuse and hasn't been occupied since 1860, but frankly, I could move in tomorrow.

33 It was initially outside the graveyard.

Chapter Six

St Andrews, Nuthurst

What Church shall we build?
A question presented to many a distant
clergyman whose mission took him to the
foothills of the Himalyas during the Indian
Raj. And in his mind's eye, there might have
emerged the image of St Andrew's of
Nuthurst. On this day at the height of summer,
I gazed across it's perfect lawns. It's tall spire
stretched up into a clear blue sky and the
baking sun cast it's shadow eastwards.

Or maybe the situation was reversed? Perhaps a returning colonial civil servant urged the diocese to develop a church in the image of one he'd seen from the hill station in Simla.

At this point in the summer of 2020, the 'lockdown' was at it's most resolutely secure. The doors to St Andrew's were firmly closed, and all guides to any church removed on account of the risk presented by the surface of paper carrying the coronovirus. For what sounds like a nightmarish world, all was remarkably peaceful. Indeed all the parishes we had visited resembled the imagined world of the returning Victorian gentleman traveller, rather than the futuristic depiction of a distant pandemic in the 1973 BBC drama *'Survivors'*.

Momentarily, it was easy to forget.

We had cycled here on two occasions over the summertime. At the first we were convinced that the pandemic would be over on our return journey, the church doors would be wide open so I could wax lyrical on the joys of the mosaic floor and stained glass windows. By our return, the brief period of normailty was rapidly evapourating and the second wave was on the way. And once again the door remained firmly shut.

Hitler didn't manage to close the Churches, neither did the Kaiser before him. In the brilliant sunlight under the clear blue sky, there were no air raid sirens and falling bombs. It was frankly perfect and that is why it was all the harder for many to come to terms with the great unseen danger that dominated 2020. But at least the patchwork of wooded hamlets were still overlooked by Church spires, acting as a reminder that normality had not all together been dispensed with.

May be it was the fact we visited on a idyllic day that gave to my untrained mind, the illusion that St Andrews wasn't particulalry old. It didn't *feel* old, it's lines too perfect, it's proportion for the Sussex countryside just too big, even transaltlantic. At first sight in was more like a church you might find in America, trying to give the impression that it was old.

How wrong I was.
St Nicholas's only connection with the modern Churches was that it had escaped the notice of Betjeman, J Charles Cox and perhaps many more. St Nicholas nestles within the Parish of St Leonards, for which the first reference was in 1287. The church – that modern construction that wouldn't be out of place in New Hampshire (or the

Himalayas), is thought to predate even this. Indeed the nave goes back to at least the 11th century. It features the tall narrow stained glass windows that are so common in our churches, which date from the 13th century and an extended chancel from the 14th. In common with Itchingfield it has a tall wooden tower which was probably errected around the same time.

As with most forest conurbations the locals appear flexible about borders, with the fine lawns of the churchyard drifting almost imperceptibly with those of their lucky neighbours.

Aside from the bricks and mortar, the appointment of the lucky encumbent clergyman was determined[34] by the Fecamp Abbey in Normandy before passing to the Bishop of Chichester, the Crown and the Bishop of London.

We strolled around the grounds that perfect Sunday afternoon and I asked my son what he thought of all these Churches we had visited during lock down.
'Well, they're all God's home, he just has a lot of them'. I didn't have a response to that.

Along with the rarely locked doors of our nation's churches, we can also attribute to Covid 19 the disappearence of the Holy Bible from our churches. Many of these buildings have witnessed tumultuous times, including civil war , the dissolution of the monastries and St Andrew's itself was right under the flight path to London during the blitz. Yet at no time did the Bible disappear from view. Until now.

Behind the locked doors the church lay quiet, the pews empty as I turned my thoughts to what might lie within those sandstone walls. A wide nave and a north vestry. To the south a rather grand porch which we happened upon before somewhat optimistically seizing the bolt of the mighty door, with all the enthusiasm of an aspirant writer in search of a subject. As was increasingly the case in this year of one main headline; 'twas not to be.

Of all the churches to which we cycled, I consider the tower of St Andrews to be the most spectacular. Timber framed and topped with a cap unique to Sussex, known appropriately enough as a Sussex cap – a blunt pyramidal roof. As the photograph illustrates it is unrelenting in it's reach for the sky.

Within it's walls lay many gems which the parishoners share with their visitors, in normal times. Many date from the Medieval era including a 13th century dug out chest, a dole cupboard and a stained glass window, a

14th century font and pews which incoporate 17th century pannelling. And finally the bells are dated 1661 and 1719 respectively. That is a fraction of what lies behind the bolted door. As I was finding, these Covid regulations were being rigidly adhered to by the obedient flock of West Sussex – which I hope brings some pleasure to the Arch Bishop of Cantebury, because it didn't to me.

34 The right of advowson – or right to appoint the encumbent member of the clergy.

Wiggonholt – One entry in the visitors book read 'such a welcoming Church – thank you for keeping your door open – so tranquil, so peaceful. Peace to all as Christmas draws near'.

Slaugham - 'Shame to see they've removed the old pews...' read at least two entries in the visitors' book. But they didn't have to sit on them every Sunday.

Staplefield- something of whiff of the continent about it, was my initial conclusion. But this feeling owed much to the work of Charles Eamer Kemp, seen here, in the murals just beneath the roof.

St Andrews, Nuthurst. Covid ensured this spectacle wasn't seen…alas.

Partridge Green, however, welcomed my family and Ian Nairn.

St Peters, Upper Beeding, at the end of a perfect summer's day.

Photograph reproduced by courtesy of Benedict C Winter

St Botolphs, utterly silent but for the sound of a lost swift.

Shoreham. Magnificence at the heart of the community.

Rudgwick
'Following the PM's statement, the church (building)
will remain locked, but the Church (people) will be
worshipping at home on Sunday mornings – join us at
10.30am for our virtual service...'

Chapter Seven

**St Michael's and All Angels,
Partridge Green.**

The Churchyard sung with grass hoppers in
the mid-day sun. And that aside, all was
peaceful as the clouds gently drifted over
Sussex.

It was difficult to assess if St Michael and
All Angels passed the 'cycle in the rain' test.
For on this day, we took shelter from the
blazing sun, under a tree at the edge of the old
church yard. Resting in the shade beside a pile
of terracotta slates, we watched the quiet
comings and goings of the parish.

Churchyards, I had thought, were the
indulgence of an age where land was plentiful
and the population sparse. A place full of

Colonels, DFC's and the occasional VC. Lichen grows on their memorials and weary travellers take their rest against the tombstone of some minor aristocrat. Perhaps in Partridge Green, land wasn't quite so scarce because, adjoining the old, was the new graveyard.

The doves of St Michael's took to the air for no apparent reason, circled the spire, and upon feeling the heat, thought better of it and returned to their roost. And with that silence returned as the clouds moved on.

In the graveyard, they had dug another row.

I had come to like the Church at Partridge Green. Like so many it was necessary to make more than one trip in the hope of finding it's doors finally flung open. In fact Partridge Green (like Rudgewick) had a lack of pretention about it. It was shamelessly built for people rather than for showing off. But then on reaching via a cycle path always puts one in the right frame of mind to see the better side of anywhere.

However, I had come to the conclusion that, like so many of my random churches, St Michaels would be just another overlooked church that if any critic picked up my book, they might well ask 'why did he choose St Michaels?' Surely the great critics of the day would never step off the train (as it was before it became a cycle path) to give their seal of approval? I was to find out.

The pigeons gazed indifferently at us from their roost, on that occasion I stepped through the front door for the first time. Once inside it is clear that the late 19th century building had been built for a growing population for althought Partridge Green is 'nowhere' it is a rather nice nowhere between London and the sea. And its population has had planning permission granted in phases to enable the unfashionable contemporary architecture of the prevailing era to crowd in around it. Mercifully, this onslaught hasn't been uniform and at the end of the day a church is nothing without a congregation.

Ironically, the Chruch was built in response to the growing population fuelled by the long gone railway station whose track I had used so extensively during this long hot summer.

I entered the church on that hot day and liberally coated my hands in the requisite hand sanitizer with which we were all so familiar. Unlike so many other churches I had visited, I could not give an account of the endless extensions and architectural clues of long forgotten archways whose impression existed in the walls, along side memorials to Crusaders and aristocrats. St Michaels was big, open, cool and welcoming. Well it might be, for it succeeded an iron mission room which had previously served the parish.

The church is carpeted in blue giving it an unusual blue haze characteristic of a RAF chapel. But it's broad nave and high ceiling gave it a relaxed and airy feel which this weary traveller enjoyed on that lazy afternoon. Like all the churches I had visited the accomodation of families was much in evidence. Neatly piled toys, notices for family meetings, photographs of Sunday school all came together to provide support, bereft of that uniform corporate image that so often proclaims that you've joined a 'family' on account of some purchase.

Back in 1890 the church on which the site stands was donated by a clergymand35 and was deigned to a 13th century style. I thought whistfully about my long suffering fictitious groundsman and how much easier his life might have been if St Michaels had been within his charge.

Overall, St Michael's is built for a congreagtion; accomodating people is its primary purpose. There is also a simplicity in its design; a disproportionately small porch gains access to the cool interior to the west of which stands the tower. To the east (or your right as you enter), you head to the chancel, via a nave of exposed brick work on which tapestries hang. And there in the east window36, the reflections of the stained glass window fall across the alter and sanctuary.

I like it and for the first time duing the course of this book, I am not alone. At some point in the history of Partridge Green an influential critic alited at the long gone railway station. Ian Nairn was a younger and more modern version of Sir John Betjeman who came to promenence in the 1960s. Unecumbered by a formal architectural qualification he avered from fashionable opinion and wrote as he saw, unwelcome or not. He coined the phrase 'subtopia' and railed against unimaginative town planning. His 'suburban' existance drew him to the conclusion that it was an unsustainable balancing act which gave him a 'deep hatred of characterless buildings and places'.37 His books were best sellers much to the irritation of trendy architects for whom sixties liberation didn't quite extend to having their own wisdom questioned. In his day Nairn was a nationally renowned critic and thus any endorsement from him, is an endorsement indeed. I have no knowledge of when he happended upon St Michaels. Or if he really arrived by train. But I do know that in 1965 the simplicity of this 'flint village church' met with his warm approval and he noted that 'other counties would have made it much fussier'. And as a visitor decades later, I found it's unfussy presence very welcoming.

35 The Rev John Goring
36 Another one by C E Kemp
37 *The Man who Fought the Planners – The Story of Ian Nairn, BBC 2014*

Chapter Eight

St Peter's, Upper Beeding.

'We held our first service today', said the lady whom I had seen stride along the gravel path in the July sunshine. She and her Labrador confidently stepped into the cool of the Church.

We were in Upper Beeding, a place with an, *other worldly* familiarity about it. It was as if all England had once been like this, before the roar of the road disturbed the tranquillity at the foot of the Downs. Perhaps sometime in the seventies I skipped school, feigning illness, only to watch some Pinewood classic that implanted this strange familiarity with Upper Beeding, in my subconscious.

Whatever, I always felt as if Upper Beeding was the England that was supposed to be. And that town planning had been a temporary aberration, before we shamefully returned to the *homely England* that had served us so well.

And there we stood, momentarily taking in the quite of the church.

That *homely England* is, to cynics, sociologists and malcontents, a figment of our imagination. And they may be right38. However, it is certainly a fact that in times of crisis, our thoughts settle on the dependable and the familiar, as if the reality of what lies ahead is too dreadful to contemplate. Indeed, in between the wars there was a surge in books that set out to define our England, not as it was, but as we might like it to have been. Bucolic book covers depicted a happy peasant stock contentedly going about their toil, eschewing modernity as they followed the plough back and forth, day in, day out, one century after the other. Their six days of labour, relieved by a Sunday spent somewhere just like this very church. And between the covers lay an account of an unchanging England as a patchwork of Parishes, rich in history, at one with nature. *The British Heritage39, I Saw Two Englands40,, In Search of England41, The Unfolding Year42* all adorn my shelves. But I feel they are a reliable history of how we needed to see ourselves, to be convinced that we should remain unified in our collective purpose. The timing of their publication was after the horrors of the Great War, and as the Second World War was looming. Would the sacrifice be worth it, all over again? And quite what had the people been asked to fight for? As yet more names were being chiselled into the war memorials, *Countryside Character*43 spelt it out for us. With contributions from Daphne Du Maurier, Henry Williamson and paintings from Peter Scott, the England all those names saved, is splayed out before us. And in the photographic section, a double page photograph of the tranquil South Downs, not a 'stone's throw' from Upper Beeding :-

Our spirits lift to the line of the sun swept downs,
(picture- unspoilt countryside)
From these hills and field, these farms and factories, the nation rallied, (picture-smiling airman – one who came home)
For the greatest conflict of all time
(picture – earnest Naval officer)
And now we look together
(picture – land girls looking into the sunset)
And the nation of tomorrow

(girl aged two, looking expectantly skyward)

One might cringe on reading this today, but between the lines they are the words of an uncomplicated people, perhaps still unsure that the cost they bore, could possibly ever be fully appreciated.

And still I could hear the gentle breeze through the tall trees in the church yard. We had crunched the gravel bordered by yew trees that stood uniformly either side of the path, only to happen upon a squat flint church overshadowed by trees. In some respects, it appeared as if the path had been planned for a grander place of worship, being both ornate and out of proportion to what awaited us. But this was no anti-climax.

Once through the porch and into the Church, the cottage like dimensions rapidly evaporated. Before us the simple nave, white washed walls, all sparsely decorated. We continued to savour the hush silence, with the afternoon sun blazing through the east window.

'It was a full house'. We looked around quizzically at the roped off pews sporting 'No Entry' signs. 'It was one family to a pew. We had thirty in total'.

'Did you do communion?'

'Oh yes, but no wine. We had masks on and went around the pews and just …' she motioned with her hand as if placing the bread in an imaginary parishioner's palm, and released her forefinger from her thumb '…popped it in their hand. No touching'.

The black Labrador yawned, and casually lay down at her feet.

We had cycled along the old railway line for twenty miles as the baking Sussex fields unfolded before us. Consequently, our muscles ached, and wind burn and a liberal coating of dust about our person made its presence felt. For a moment I wished that I could have laid down as unselfconsciously as the dog.

'When will we get back to normal?' we asked, mindful of the fact that all our Church services had been online for the last four months.

'Who knows' replied our host, whom I deduced to be the vicar. 'I was supposed to be marrying my son this year'. Lives on hold in more ways than one. Of course, we shall emerge from this, but its effect will be felt for a generation. Will there be stained glass windows depicting the sacrifice of the staff of the NHS, or stone memorials like those that followed the wars? At least the war failed to close down the church buildings and they were relied upon by a frightened populace in need of reassurance. Like everything else, our church lived on, on the internet. I expected it had been the same for St Peters.

Upper Beeding is situated on the northern end of the River Adur gap in the heart of the South Downs. The site is a bridging point over the river to Bramber, home of the famous castle, passed in a heartbeat when in a car, its people and parish once separated by the river. Such factors once made a vast difference to the communities' existence. Indeed, such divisions even aroused suspicions of neighbours whom they could see but struggled to meet. All different now as we cycled over the bridge, initially unaware that in doing so, we were passing from Bramber into a completely different village. Perhaps I was distracted by the lady paddle boarder whom we shared the time of day with, only to see her silhouette raise a hand in the setting sun, as the South Downs Link passed over the northern reaches of the river. Catching the tide, we had been advised was essential. Given the distance she had travelled, I would say she had been successful.

Ofcourse, being unaware that one was passing from Bramber to Upper Beeding did nothing to aid the search for the church. The locals would find the thought amusing, that one can actually get lost in somewhere so small.

With the smell of cooking from the Indian restaurant throwing temptation in my way, we pedalled on until we happened upon the sign guiding us to the church.

Upper Beeding had originally been known simply as 'Beeding'. Indeed, the ecclesiastical parish retains the name, or the much larger 'mouthful' of 'The Parish of Beeding and Bramber with St Botolph's'. This delightful lack of abbreviation, so loved by town clerks, probably helps to keep some jobs exclusive to the community.

St Peters has not been without other challenges down the centuries. In 1307 it was all but completely demolished. What we see is the rebuilt church, replete with a tower, blessed with six bells. And long before the surrounding development it had been a Benedictine Priory. Even now it is not difficult to picture in the mind's eye, the remote refuge it must have been. Indeed Beeding (as it was then) had an entirely separate neighbour known as the hamlet of Sele, which was destined to be engulfed by the very modest growth of Upper Beeding. The current village centre is equidistant between the two Saxon settlements. Indeed,

Saxon Beeding was closer to the modern development known as Dacre Gardens, whilst Saxon Sele was closer to the Church. For that reason it was initially known as Sele Priory. And the monks back in the thirteenth century were not narrow in their vision for they decided to set up a mission further up county. Lower Beeding, was the name given to their upper mission base. At a time when most travel was on foot, to have the extremity of the parish ten miles away, must have tested their fortitude but even so, it remained part of the same parish until Victorian times.

'And we do have a Pugin light'

'Do you indeed?'

'Oh yes, it's around here'

We followed our host briefly to the aisle, and there strung from the roof was an ornate light, like a regal crown. Musing for a moment, our host added, 'it doesn't work'. Why should it? Surely it is enough to be a Pugin? Having made his presence felt on these journeys, and in circumstances in which I felt I should offer some knowledgeable endorsement, it was time to find out more. I quickly discovered that:-

Pugin was one of the most entertaining men of the last century. And after his death the doctors said that in the forty years of his life he had done enough work to last a man a century. 44

Well, that will do.

The entertaining side of his character is particularly attractive. It is manifested in one who could be excused for being insufferably self-important as are those who've achieved far less. His austere and eccentric upbringing at the hands of his formidable mother allowed numerous eccentricities to emerge on being set free – indeed, his dress was distinctive, to say the least. Imagine turning up on a building site today and leaning against a cement mixer to address the assembled trades, whilst dressed as a sailor, replete with 'sailors' jacket, loose pilot trousers, jack boots and a wide-awake-hat' 44(a).

Indeed!

None of which stopped him from achieving propriety and fame whilst leaving his architectural mark upon St Chads R C Cathedral Birmingham along with a swathe of places of worship across the Midlands, Berkshire, and London before satisfying himself with St Giles in Cheadle, to such an extent that he built his own house beside it.

And here it is, hanging in St Peters in Upper Beeding; small wonder the vicar pointed it out, whether it was working or not. It was becoming difficult to escape the conclusion that the 'ordinary churches' of Sussex (whatever they maybe), harboured some unique treasures. Were these housed in a Cathedral, one might have to pay for entrance, and find oneself surrounded by busloads of tourists holding their mobile phone to the heavens, whilst beaming for the benefit of unknown 'virtual friends'.

We would like to have spent more time at St Peters, but somewhere so close to the end of the South Downs Link, is inevitably, a long ride from home.

My impression of St Peters, is one of eccentric dimensions. The path to the porch is grander than to many urban Cathedrals, yet whilst the building is smaller it's human dimensions are entirely welcoming. This curiosity, perhaps has something to do with the ancient nature of the Christian community gathered around the River Adur. Now dating Churches, is never easy but at the time of the foundations, the population of the UK was roughly equivalent to that of central London. The monks lived as hermits on two flagons of ale and a loaf of bread, and the only familiar aspect of their lives, which they would recognise today, is the routine of today's monks who live by the Rule of St Benedict. Other than that, the complications of modern living have little in common with such tribulations as the 12th Century was presented with. Their main challenge has long been overcome, and that is presented by the craft of building. Whilst this building is a testament to their craftsmanship, the design of all Churches is limited by technological advancement. In different centuries, men built in different ways. Now English men are famous for loving their sheds, but few of us are particularly creative with them, and when we are, unsuccessful attempts at ornate features, generate wastes, ill temper and even trip to A & E. Shed man, is little more than an advanced cave man. Whilst today the power tools of suburbia scream away, their long-suffering families seldom see much emerge that earns them any familial respect for a moment, let alone centuries. But bereft of a source of power, the craftsman of our churches toiled away perfecting shapely door ways, arches, pillars and windows. The tools they used were basic. Consequently, the older the age, the smaller the church. The ancient craftsman did not know how to safely put up high walls or safely fix a high roof over a wide building. But with perseverance they learnt. And without St Pauls there would have been no Centre Point… perhaps not the best example.

We turned our back on St Peters and made our way back along the path. Just under the apex of the arch is a 'crude' (or just ancient?) sculpture of what appears to be someone administering communion, just one outstanding question justifying a return journey.

I had so wanted to attend evensong at St Peters. Indeed, at the outset I thought I would catalogue the visits made to locked down churches in their silence and conclude each section when the nation had been freed. A celebration of our collective emergence, if you like. As with my initial plans to write literally about evensong, this too was being buffeted by events. There was talk of a 'second wave', to which I was as sceptical, as I was of that thing called Covid 19 when mentioned at the start of the year. I wasn't alone. At our very first service in January, there seemed to be far more concern about Brexit. That sermon was delivered in the quiet mists of January. As the Church baked in the blazing July sunshine, I wondered if this might be the year, we all 'ate out words'.

Whatever the outcome of our year, I feel that ultimately, the parishioners of St Peters will beat the gravel path and pass under the Porch, to be met by that familiar hush. The no entry signs will fall, the pews will be packed, the peace exchanged and communion will be carried out by a clergy who do not wear masks.

Ultimately.

38 And they may be wrong.
39 Multiple contributors, published by Odhams Press
40 H V Morton 1942
41 H V Morton 1927 Methuen
42 Hockley Clarke 1947
43 Multiple contributors, Blandford Press 1946.
44 Augustus Welby Pugin, by John Betjeman. BBC broadcast.
44(a). Benjamin Ferrey

Chapter Nine

St Botolph's, The South Downs.

At last, there is the promise of rain, as the South Downs rise up before us. The birds can sense a change in the atmosphere as the folding hillsides are slowly obscured by a creeping mist. Anytime now.

We are approching St Botolphs, named after the patron saint of 'boundaries'. I confess to not knowing that we had such a saint or indeed that boundaries really warranted one. Be that as it may, boundaries are linked to farming which makes more sense in this truly rural parish.

The lane winds and then starts to climb. To our left, behind a flint wall the church tower rises above us, and there it is, as it has been since Saxon times. Set in an expansive churchyard, bordered at the opposite end by tall trees that have bent ever so slightly northwards, in the gathering breeze from the coast.

I open the stubborn gate that drags along the dusty floor. There before us the well worn path leads, eventually, to the porch entrance to the church.

St Botolphs achitectural journey, is the journey of our times, albeit one where it was shaped by local events. At the outset a navigable river played a large part in determining its location. As the population grew so did the church, from an aisleless building with a nave to one that finally gained a tower in the thirteenth century. And then the river silted up and the population fell. The loss of a crossing point that had been used for a thousand years, contributed to a further fall. In the eighteenth century the population doubtless had other worries than the deterioration of what we, from the comfort of food stuffed supermarkets, consider to be the sacrilegious deterioration of pretty buildings. And so, the aisle fell into disrepair and with an insufficient parish to address the decline, the adjacent arcade was demolished leaving three blank arches in the north wall, that are clearly visible to this day.

Whatever the historic trials and tribulations of the parishoners, they have left behind a peaceful setting, enjoyed largely by passing tourists and a resident tame crow. The rustics have long gone and the slopes of the Downs face the sun awaiting either rain or the arrival of a tractor festooned with some incomprehensible implement that stops the occasional traffic.

Sitting in a pew, I took in the scene; it certainly looked and felt like the oldest building I had enterrred on this journey[45]. Above me a confused swift made its graceful way around the ceiling as I transfer my gaze between the Jacobean pulpitt and its flight. I am sitting in a parish, perhaps a little redundant now, that can trace it's roots back to 956. It has seen of the movement of the river, the loss of a bridge, cement works and railway and remains a deeply spirtual place. The precise date of the nave is unknown over and above it originating in the Saxon era. Although administered by the Historic Chruches Trust it is still part of the The Parish of Beeding and Bramber with Botolphs. This is a fully functioning parish rather than a collection of buidlngs well suited to adorning picture postcards. Indeed St Botolphs is listed as one of the 500 holiest places in England. It has witnessed the arrival of the Normans who excersised their prerogative as conquerors to rename the church. Upon considering St Botolph to be too obscure they simply changed it to St Peter. Alas the local Angles were famously awkward and St Botolphs lingered on in their collective memory only to return as soon as decently (or safely) possible. This occured sometime in the 14th century and possibly as a consequence of continuous mischeaviuos reference to St Botlphs, the local village adopted the name for good measure as well.

It's size and simplicity probaby added to the feeling of peace, but in its day St Botolphs was considered rather grand being constructed of expensive stoen rather in contrast to the wooden buildings that surrounded the parish. And naturally, none of those sported glass windows which were then asrtonomically expensive.

I strolled quietly down the nave and happened upin the stone font. This is unusually deep because babies were baptised by full emersion. Pitty the stonemason…and the baby.

Outside the wind had passed and so had the threat of rain. The tame crow walked a couple of foot behind us as we picked up our cycles. My son threw him a tomato which the crow promptly pick up, cocked his head and trumphantly flew away with.

Minutes later, we were back on the cycle track heading for home.

45 Actually it isn't – that credit goes to St Peters.

Chapter Nine

St Mary's de Haura, Shoreham.

The wind ushered the clouds along and gave the first hint that this had been a blistering season, that was preparing to leave our shores.

It was late afternoon, the time of day when passers by made their determined way home, oblivious to the family sat in the shade. The shadow drew back as the cloud passed and St Marys de Haura was bathed in sunlight once more.

We sat in the grounds of the church, looking up at its tower as young people ambled by and parted as the bells rang out.

We would shortly be on our way, but St Mary's makes you want to stay. It is situated, appropriately, in Church Square in Shoreham. The square is a back water to a back water, Shoreham being ancillary to the city of Brighton. The square is bordered by a narrow street on the other side of which, are the homes of the well to do. Charity and antique shops are shoulder to shoulder with artisan bakers and Hector's café. Things are definitely *different,* the closer you get to Brighton, and I wouldn't have it any other way. And this micro-community is served and overshadowed by St Mary's, right at it's centre. And it is comparable to a cathedral, yet those who travel by car or train could easily pass by, oblivious to it's existance. Only the light aircraft from the nearby airfield would see its splendour in persective. But for the majority of hurried travellers, Brighton beckons, whilst St Mary's gently casts its shadow around the square, as it all goes on around it.

Occasionally a vehicle will navigate its way around the perimeter of the square. And St Mary's and its garden remain peaceful, well used, even worn. Families sit at the benches that lie inside the perimeter wall, and watch the world go by. This is not a church that's purpose is to charge you entry and invite you to circle its ancient stonework in search of 'selfies'; it feels that it serves a purpose. And inside a message from the Reverand Ann Waizeneker greets the visitor thus:-

It's a great privelege that so many people come here for so many reasons; from joyful occasions, to those times when we turn to God in despair, and those times when we are asking questions about faith. So whatever your reasons for being here, welcome…

But as with so many of our churches, its roots are far from peaceful, for it would probably never have been, but for the Norman Conquest. And those roots can be seen around the churchyard, for there amidst the leaning grave stones may protrude a stone outcrop; evidence of some wall or foundation whose purpose has long since past.

It is always difficult to state what happened so long ago, but we do know that in 1066 Britain was successfully invaded by William the Conqueror. With William came Philip De Braose who did their worst in Hastings, to the eastern extremity of the county (and much closer to France, making the sea crossing so much shorter). It is Philip's son, William De Braose whom we have to thank for St Mary's De Haura, for he was it's founder. Having campaigned in the Crusades he returned to England in 1103, and now looks down upon the congregation from the De Braose window, in which he is depicted in stained glass, resplendent in the armour that saw him through Jerusalem.

Having passed it's 900th birthday, the grounds around the church look like nature has had an equal hand at the conclusion of this particularly hot summer. At the South end of the churchyard, the wall gives way to the pedestrianised part of the town; more charity shops and an Italian restaurant sporting the flags of Italy, Ferrrari and Great Britain which flutter over the seated area as the diners on the terrace soak up the last of the summer sun, and the oppurtunity to dine, for there is alreay talk of another wave of coronavirus.

Back in 1100 AD the church consisted of the lower stage of the tower and a shorther nave[46] and a chancel[47]. For all their sense of permanence, churches have been under a process of evolution from the outset and St Mary's is no exception with the enlargement of the nave with additional aisles, and the chancel being redesigned by the end of the 12th century. By the medieval period the nave had fallen into disrepair.

Outside a travelling Australian is entertaining the diners with a didgereedoo and a kettle drum. The unamplified tunes gently drift around Church Square as an elderley gentlemen tends one particular grave in the church yard. I had tried to catch his eye, but so intent was he that the oppourtunity never arose. If it was a family grave it must have been his distant ancestors for the area looked centuries old. I felt therefore that it was more likely to be a local dignatry whose memorial had fallen to his charge. But who? There was something of note in an ancient grave where the soil was being turned and flowers planted hundreds of years later. He remained undisturbed by me and by the passing pedestrians, as ferral pigeons drifted overhead before settling on the church roof.

The picture of the nave looking towards the altar is in the picture section of this book. In the middle of the aisle is a sign forbidding visitors from going any further. We will not forget these times. As I turned from as near as I could get to the altar, I looked down the aisle to where the font now lies, under the tower crossing as a shaft of sunlight illuminated the Norman stone work. I was all alone in the silence as I surveyed the scene. I don't know for how long and one might say there is nothing unusual about this. Indeed there can't be for the sun must have illuminated the font many times over hundreds of years. But I was struck by that rare moment of peace, as that simple artefact, carved with different designs on its four sides became the focal point of my attention. Indeed following the Synods dictact to remove all paperwork (including Bibles) and any other surfaces on which the virus might settle, there was little else to distract the attention. It was probably as it would have appeared to the original congregation.

Back in church, I briefly took a pew. To my left there are sunken arches in the north aisle which gave an ancient monstic feel to my untrained eye. Within each arch was strung a painting[48]. Slowly I moved back down the nave (or central aisle, if you like).

And then the bell rang and I heard someone else enter the church behind me.

I stood briefly along side the font, under the tower, which is supported by four arches capable of taking it's massive weight for nearly a complete millenia. These are all part of the original Norman church of 1100AD.

I was sorry that I couldn't have attended evensong here, but if it was anything like our own church, numbers were strictly regulated and a booking could only take place online. With all these churches I had gained the impression that at each point in the history of the tumultuous year 2020, they were taking the covid 19 precautions with the utmost seriousness.

The chancel49, the approach to which was cordonned off, is a mere 800 years old. This consists of three levels, having of both Norman and and Gothic arches, with the chancel and it's aisles supported by flying buttresses. It is these, which give say Salisbury Cathedral or Notre Damne their distinctive look. Yet Shoreham is considered a parish church, for which such architectural features are usually reserved for the grander places of worship.

St Mary's feels that it 'oozes' with history and deserves a book all too itself. Consequently I have been cautious of writing about these deeply cherished places of worship, for fear of incurring the wrath of some retired Headmaster amongst the congregation whom, bereft of books to mark, rounds on my modest offering's short comings for wont of precision and accuracy. If offered a pre caining homily, I can but reply that at the outset I simply sought to record little more than the *feel* of a church. Dates, you can find elsewhere, but in 2020 when the congregation needed the peace of the Lord, more than many preceding years, our

Churches served their purpose admirably. In all of these Churches, whenever I sat in solitude, I never fealt alone. And that, perhaps, is the most important fact of all.

The columns are a mix of styles; the architects down the ages caring little for uniformity, choosing to mix styles such that the eye can settle on round or octagonal columns. The latter style is shared with no lesser cathedral than Canterbury, but in a flourish of creativity some of the columns are decorated with stone leaves, which appear to be blown by the wind. And one of those columns has an ornate cross, the history of which is unclear. However it is thought to commemorate the visit of the patriarch of Jerusalem.

'Grand', as I feel St Mary's is, it has a very worn and lived in feel, which adds to the sense of homeliness.

During this whole period, everything has been the same, but not quite the same, somehow. The unseen enemy around us is so well disguised that false senses of security abound, and there are times when we even doubt the viruses existance. Until the infection rate rises. And still the sun shone and the roads were quieter, and once we thought it was over, how quickly we got back to normal. Yet at the outset, as the headlines prepared us for a summer in isolation, a picture appeared of a man in central London carrying a placard which read *Jesus Is Coming Soon*. In any other age he might have been considered a mild eccentric, but having been failed to some degree, by our collective logic, his views didn't seem so out of place. But on this day, face masks and hand sanitiser apart, we were nearly back to normal. And the man with the didgeridoo played on.

Had I been able to reach the south chancel aisle, I would have been greeted by three carvings of the Green Man; a reminder that we haven't always been a Chrtistain nation and the conversion from paganism wasn't overnight. The effigy depicts an old man with branches growing out of his mouth and vegetation for hair. A fertility figure and celebration of nature, his presence isn't uncommon in churches despite his tenuous link with Christianity. Could it have been necessary to ease the transition to faith, to put something in our churches with which uncertain Pagans could readily identify? By contrast there are two brasses a little further along the aisle of two inhabitants in prayer. Their clothing is 14th century, typical of wealthy merchant folk, for by then Shoreham was the main port to the continent. Was the transition to Christianity connsidered complete and they, by virtue of their faith and wealth, rewarded with a burial on the floor of the Church? Equal as we may be in the eyes of God, we appear to have always had regard for status, I fear.

The inevitable corollory of an imposed[50] social order, is dissent. And as we see in the modern age, that dissent manifests itself in many unrelated causes. For evidence of this, we need not look in the lofty tomes of academic journals gathering dust in reference libraries. The real chronicle of our times is sprayed on public walls and scratched into school desks, for graffiti has never been subject to peer pressure or public censure. If someone were to leave their message on St Mary's I would join the calls for corporal punishment (although forgiveness would ofcourse be the correct thing to do). But graffitti that is hundreds of years old has gained a certain respectability, even if it must have caused a stir at the time, when the local ne'er-do-well surreptitiously took out his chizel to make his feeling fealt. Shoreham's graffiti dates back to the 17th century and is deeply cut into the south chancel piers. It appears that some parishoners did not approve of the imminent arrival of the Rector of Southwark in 1670. The same body of people may shortly thereafter have departed these very shores to establish a puritan existance in the United States. Indeed two years later a New Shoreham was established on Block Island, New England. The graffiti bearing the date, crude pictures of a home and their initials, may have been their parting farewell.

We have made a number of visits to Shoreham over the summer, perhaps an inevitability of being at the end of the cycle track. Be that as it may, the visits have always been welcoming. Church Square has an air of calm about it. On Fridays there is a clear route taken by men and boys towards a local mosque. Like boys eveywhere, they kick balls and climb walls. Like Father's everywhere they bring their sons into line and move on. Worship is not nearly so straight forward eveywhere, not least in the Middle East where going to Church exposes you to risk of assualt, being shot at or kidnapped. My peaceful meanderings amongst the random chruches of West Sussex, are in contrast with those of so many others around the world for whom such an act poses a risk to their life.

Quietly and without fear of intrusion I meander down the nave towards the shaft of light over the font and the exit behind. I pick up an order of prayer marked *'Please take this leaflet with you once you have handled it as part of infection control'*. The second page recites part of the Gospel of Matthew, '*Come to me, all you that are weary and carry heavy burdens, and I will give you rest*'51. In the transept to my right, a lady had crept in and sat alone. It was time for me to leave.

Once the door closed behind me the air filled with the gentle hubbub of conversation and passing pedestrians. A light aircraft passes overhead, gently drifting into Shoreham airport over the nearby River Adur. That pilot will be treated to the sight of St Mary's from above. On looking down the buiding will look like a cross, the cross bar being formed out of the two transepts which I had just passed. In medieval times they were used as chapels, illuminated by Norman windows in each. But in 1947 the north transept was ordered as a memorial chapel, and that chapel remains a place of private prayer to this day.

Unlike Covid, we had been aware that the last war was coming for sometime. Mindful of the diminishing oppurtunities to survey our home land, the author Richard Wyndham set out to have regard to the Southern England he loved so much and like many, would soon be leaving. In his book Titled *One Last Look*52, Wyndahm happened upon Shoreham and described it thus:-

The coast road west from Brighton is now linked to Shoreham by seven miles of stucco-and-brick cottages – but by nothing else. There is, and always will be, a fundamental difference between these two towns. It is the difference between a sea that is bathed in and a sea that is sailed by ships. You notice the change as soon as you reach Portslade: instead of piers and promenades and fun fairs, you find cranes and high smoking chimneys; timber yards, coal stacks, petroleum tanks, grimy brick ware-houses, black tarred wharfes, the sound of riveting, and the smell of gas.

Perhaps not quite the buccolic idyll to give a weary combatant on a distant shore a sentimental glow about his homeland. But his parting in 1944 from a port bracing itself for D-Day may have been indifferent to astheitics, as many a nervous soldier strolled the streets, waiting for a break in the weather and praying for a safe passage, perhaps even bowing his head in the north transept and asking for God's blessing in what lay ahead.

We are, it seems, always destined to face challenge and at this moment mine was only to find the energy to turn my wheels northward for the journey home. And such a modest challenge is a blessing indeed.

That morning I had woken early and found the cobwebs strung between the blades of grass, carried a heavy dew in that sharp cold air; the first sign, I fealt, that whilst it might have been high summer, there was one part of the day's cycle into which the autumn had already spread, even if only briefly. Soon it was burnt off and a warm day ensued, but on the cycle ride down I had heard the gentle falling of acorns. After 40 miles of cycling, I turned in that night and the sounds my mind played back to me, in my half state of consciousness before succumbing to a deep sleep, were of falling acorns, and church bells.

46 Probably
47 The area before that most sacred part of the Church, the altar that lies under the East window
48 Not technically an icon, but very much in the style of one.
49 The area before that most sacred part of the Church, the altar that lies under the East window
50 and unjust?
51 Matthew 11 verse 28.
52 Published in 1940 in an uncertain Britain, it was also titled *South Eastern Survey* and was republished in 2019 by Batsford Books as *Surrey, Sussex & Kent 1939*. But perhaps *One Last Look* best sums the book up, as that is precisely what it was.

Chapter Ten

Holy Trinity, Rudgwick.

Storm Alex had made his presence felt. Gone were the balmy still days of autumn, the chimney smoke rising skyward and the gently dropping acorns. There was a power hose from the heavens and a sheet of driving rain. The path that only a week ago was still baked hard from months of hot sun was a continuous puddle. The few other cyclists on the South Downs Link were far from happy; and there's no avoiding the rain. When it pours you are going to get wet; resistance is futile. When you are drenched to the skin, its nothing like as uncomfortable as cowering away from the rain in a semi dry state.

And so I cycled on, alone amongst the fallen leaves and the mud. The sound of traffic was rapidly replaced by the sound of wind through the trees and my wheels in the water.

And on to Rudgwick. The unseen village, most of which lies in Sussex, but some lies in Surrey, I am sure. May be this makes a difference to the value of your house: may be not. But Rudgwick is a proper village, to the point of being a tiny bit 'hick'. In fact there's more 'hick' in wooded Surrey than many a stockbroker would care to admit. And in Rudgwick there apears to be a disproportionate number of Land Rovers that are used for more than merely taking the children to school. And, I happen to know, a shire horse and a steam fair. And a mix of properties, lived in by locals and built when the rest of the world was very precious about mundane seventies architecture.

But by and large the world speeds by at a horrendous speed *en route* to Guildford, and no one goes to Rudgwick. No one ever went to Rudgwick, not H V Morton, not Sir John Betjeman or even Richard Wyndham. Ruardean, Rudston, Rufford, Rufforth, Rugby, Ruislip, Rumburgh and on reads the index to *Collins Guide to English Parish Churches*. But alas Rudgwick has been overlooked. And Rudgwick Church could still be overlooked, as it lies behind the village pub. And unlike the pub in Slaugham, it hasn't been knocked down, allowing the Church to dominate the village. Instead, you enter the churchyard through a gap in some narrow cottages, charming in themselves, beside the public house. I had to wonder how many worshippers at evensong had paused, pictured a pint being pulled, briefly succumbed to the belief that there was time, only to re-emerge long after the verger had turned out the lights.

I had cycled passed the church several times before finding that gap between the pub and cottages (I didn't, I hasten to add, visit *The Kings Head*), despite seeing the church clearly from the road. Indeed it is on a hilll, surrounded by trees. And when walking around the churchyard, you can, at one point, spy a fine view of the unfolding Sussex countryside to the south.

The Parish had taken the Prime Minister's announcement most seriously and did not simply remove paperwork and provide hand santizer, but had locked the church completely. And to a drenched cyclist, a church door that is locked feels very firmly locked indeed. But wisely the renovation due, was under way, scaffolding had been errected and sundry building materials were piled up to the rear of the church. The Church tower had looked out over the village since 1200, and so there had probably been many renovations down the centuries. All entirely justified and the pandemic presented the ideal oppurtunity to get on with them. But with only the incessant drip from the scaffolding that landed on a sheet of corregated iron, to break the silence, one felt very alone.

On walking round the church it is clear that this is another substantial place of worship, serving what was then a very small, largely rural community. Even today it has less than 3,000 inhabitants, yet the church wouldn't be out of place in a large town.

Occasional gravestones of the grand protrude the vegetation along with a minor statue of a solemn angel, so loved by the Victorians. All in a rural parish on a Ridge53, whose populace earned their living on the land, the brickworks and until 1965 at its own railway station. Today, farming is highly mechanised and the village has lost its railway station but gained a presevation society. One gets the impression that as a community, bereft of 'airs and graces', Rudgwick works. But I am no sociologist (thankfully).

It is perhaps shocking (to some at least), that a parish so close to the stockbroker belt should have once been described thus:-

"And they say that there are in this parish no major estates, nor any merchants, but the parishioners live off the land by their own labour."[54]

It is a curious thing, being as frequently mistaken as only I know how, but in many of the parishes I have visited, my crudely developing amateur historian's 'feel' for a place has led me to the conclusion that the inhabitants were particularly affluent. A conclusion reached on the basis of their parish churches. But I have almost always been wrong. Perhaps the devotions of the historically malnourished and illiterate are not to be underestimated; then or now.

And on I strolled around the dripping church yard, marvelling at another church. One which had all the trappings of permanance, yet one that, I had long learned from these excursions, was under a constant state of evolution. Indeed, the tower had two porches at the turn of the last century. The one remaining appeared to have been recently renderred as part of the current rennovations. And though the tower is ancient and impressive, it appears that it is built from the material of an even older tower that was pulled down in the name of progress. Indeed that 12th Century tower lasted but a hundred years before the current tower replaced it, and rather grand it is too. Within lies the font – made of Horsham marble[55] and dating back to the 12th century and thus acquaitned with the original tower, and now laying claim to being one of the oldest artefacts in the church. The south wall may be one of the oldest parts of the church and is probably as old as the tower with further additions in the 14th and 15th century. Such detail doubtless matters to some, but the upshot is a rather grand building that leaves one with the impression that much more went on here than history has chosen to record. But it's only an impression.

And still the rain fell, and my goodness it was chilly as I waded through the drenched grass of the churchyard, whence I happened upon a Norman Apse. Now the Norman period spanned 1076 – 1075. And it was perfectly round, as aspes tend to be – easily giving the impression that it could only have been created by modern craftsmen whom benefit from CGI's[56]. And as with so many angular buildings it looked both a tiny bit out of place, and simutaneously pleasing on the eye.

And I shivered and contemplated the bizarre pleasure that this journey had given me. And there is little doubt that had I made these forays up and down the cycle tracks of

Sussex in any other year, then this book would have been a very different one. Alas 2020 was the year was the year of the coronovirus and it had, in some ways, as big an impact on us as practically any event in human history. When first it was announced the unseeing, unfeeling invisible threat conjured up a feeling of unreality. That early spring morning when the congregation was unable to indulge in in coffee and biscuits, seemed serious enough. Someone whispered in my ear, 'well 1400 people die each day anyway' and there were the first signs of such mutiny as those in courdroys and quilted jackets are inclined to muster upon depravation of caffine. That felt a long time ago now. In the intervening months I had been wet, hot, cold, down right filthy but constantly happy. The quiet solitude of these churches had been a blessing in a very unusual year, during which I had learnt that my sentimental view of the church as an unchanging building, reassuring in it's familiarity was, well, just sentiment. And this view goes back, like so many things, to one's childhood.

---

53 The village, if it could be titled such in 1210, was originally called Regwick or farm on the ridge. Long before this, the bones of it original inhabitant, a rare dinosuar – the *Polacanthus Rudgwickensis* set themselves in the soil, and

commenced their rest until 1985, whereon they were finally discovered and
moved to the natural history museum.

54 The Nonae Rolls

55 also known as Petworth marble or indeed Sussex marble.

56 Computer generated images, apparently.

Chapter Eleven

St Johns, Broadbridge Heath.

My first memory of church was from the village in which I grew up in rural Yorkshire in the 1970s. The congregation was drawn from a village of 1500, half of whom worked on farms and had been there forever, and the 'newcomers'. I was one of these and in retrospect, the old village might have had concerns that the old order was in danger of being disturbed.

The place where the two came together was in the church, on a hill, with a Norman tower and a much newer nave with large windows giving a glimpse of the distant Yorkshire wolds. Through the East window any sunlight was interupted by large yew trees which were planted on account of their poisonous berries which deterrred neighbouring farmers from grazing their livestock on consecrated ground.

The hymns were traditional and accompanied by an elderly lady on the organ called Freda. Freda had been there forever and nobody really knew why she had been appointed organist. At the same time nobody had the courage to raise the question. There were two distinct charcteristics of Freda as an organist. The first was an almost child like curiosity of what might happen if you pressed a key that wasn't on the music score. This might be mildly amusing mid sermon but curiosity invariably got the better of Freda mid way through *Rock of Ages* when the 1763 classic suddenly seemed to have been taken over by free style jazz musicians. We learned to pretend not to notice. The other charactristic was a most undignified way of throwing her leg over the organ stool, about which I shall say no more.

Along with Freda were a multitude of farm hands and at various times the occupiers of three manor houses along the main street, all of whom had the right to consider themselves to be the squire.

As children we were stuffed into our Sunday best and expected to be seen and not heard. If anyone asked how you were doing at school it was always 'very well', which given the accuracy of the reply was, in some cases, inappropriate on consecrated ground.

Things hadn't changed and weren't going to change, not least church services, which in the quiet of the English countryside had a kind of unchallenging reassurance.

And then the Californians came. I don't know who they were but they made an impression as rather pleasant people strumming guitars and wearing sandals. As their sunny contenance gazed upon the massed congregation, they apologised for their slow speech which was a development of living in warmer climes where it was simply too hot to speak quickly. The rain continued to lash against the windows as the congregation shivered. And then they brought out the tabourines.

I was young, but old enough to realize that the lack of audience participation, particulalry when it came to waving your arms, was indicative of the fact that English countryfolk just weren't ready to let their hair down.

It was a most uncomfortable experience and the following Sunday I was happy to return to Ploughing the Fields and Scattering, not for any musical or theological virtue, but just so that you could rest knowing what would happen next; nothing.

The memory stayed with me for years until having married into a family of Baptists I found myself sat alongside my mother in law, in a church service during which they played
Bob Marley. The ghosts of another age came back to me in a flash, not least as I had long had ingrained in me that church was a place of one organ, some songs, an old building and some slightly posh people.

But the Lord moves in mysterious ways and for all my years of mumbling through the Lord's prayer, gazing out of the window (a tradition, for good or ill, but still a tradition), may be there was nothing to fear in tambourines. A sermon in which I was told that we were God's representatives on earth lead me to grow distinctly hot under the collar. In that case he wasn't being particualrly well represented by me.

All the foregoing thoughts must have been in the back of my mind as we took part in the Ride 'n' Stride Charity for the Historic Churches Trust. We simply picked the Churches on the basis of ticking off as many as we could without using main roads. Some were manned, some were not, some were in town, others remote. Some welcoming, others empty but blessed with a tea tray and orange juice to help yourself. And with that we thought we'd go to St Johns in Broadbridge Heath, for no other reason than they are bound to be open because they throw themselves at everything.

Unlike all the other churches in this book, St Johns is thoroughly modern; a steel structure lined with wood, and tent shaped. It is certainly striking with each side of the tent being made largely of glass and so very bright and welcoming. For 1963 this was quite an innovation which is intended to resemble the 'tent of meeting' from the Old Testament. All a long way from Freda's organ, indeed I am not sure if they have one. In fact eveytime we have been there there's been a drum kit, electric keyboards and naturally guitars (thankfully not a tambourine – even now; the memory). And yet there is no denying that those Californians of Yorkshire might have found it easier to arouse this congregation.

And so we cycled on to St John's which appeared a hive of activity.
I might have found it easier to write about the previous structure; a church made of iron and wood put down in 1904, it lasted 53 years before being declared unsafe. It was like a tabernacle with pews and an alter, a

conventional spire and just a little bit dowdy on the inside. I felt as if I didn't need check if either of St Johns buildings made ever made it into the *Collins Guide to English Churches.* It didn't seem to matter. The church is always full.

Each year they have a camp in nearby fields in which generation after generation of children have grown up – our son has certainly had the time of his life there. All a long way from children being seen and not heard.

We eased up as a lady lugging a branch over her shoulder emerged to greet us warmly. Soon there was a procession of volunteers who had been tidying the garden to welcome us too. I was getting nervous as they might have thought we'd volunteered and then felt uneasy once again, having volunteered for very little in my life.

The impression left by St Johns was of a particularly friendly welcome and yet the curious thing was, they weren't even taking part in the Ride 'n' Stride.

I pondered these things as I sped along the lanes of Sussex. I could not avoid the conclusion that many children will emerge from their time at St Johns (and indeed all these churches), with the most secure of memories. Life moves at a pace and it may be years before they revisit these memories, perhaps not until they are parents themselves. But remembering people and events witnessed as children, and then revisiting them years later through the eyes of an adult can provide very welcome reassurance, that we are not alone.

A Prayer for all those affected by **Coronavirus**

Keep us, good Lord,
under the shadow of your mercy.
Sustain and support the anxious,
be with those who care for the sick,
and lift up all who are brought low;
that we may find comfort
knowing that nothing can separate us from your love
in Christ Jesus our Lord. Amen.

Psalm 62: 5-6

For God alone my soul waits in silence,
  for my hope is from him.
⁵ He alone is my rock and my salvation,
  my fortress; I shall not be shaken.

Isaiah 43: 1-2

Do not fear, for I have redeemed you;
  I have called you by name, you are mine.
² When you pass through the waters, I will be with you;
  and through the rivers, they shall not overwhelm you.

Matthew 11:28 King James Version

²⁸ Come unto me, all ye that labour and are heavy laden, and I
will give you rest.

From the Front door of St Michael's & All Angels,
Partridge Green.

Thank you...for buying this book and I hope that you enjoyed the read.

It may have been that there wasn't a lot to do in 2020, but I certainly enjoyed cycling around all these churches and writing the book. In fact, lockdown or not, I would very much like to do it again.

You may have noticed that the price of the book is what marketing people call 'competitive'. This is because it is being sold without any author royalties being included in the sale price.

Instead, I have enough faith in the human condition to believe that asking for a contribution to a charity via the QR code on the next page, has every bit as much chance of raising money for a worthy cause (in this case the Salvation Army), as putting up the price and then donating all the royalties to charity. In this case you decide the royalty, based upon what you can afford, how much you liked the book or just how much you are comfortable with paying. Either way, I am grateful if you just got as far as this page.

If you are unfamiliar with QR codes then the Just Giving page is at: -
Nigel C Winter is fundraising for The Salvation Army (justgiving.com)

Best wishes,

Nigel.

The Salvation Army is a Christian Church & registered Charity working in 130 countries worldwide and is one of the largest and most diverse providers of social welfare in the world. In the UK and Republic of Ireland this work includes more than 800 Salvation Army social service centres and Community churches. We provide unconditional friendship, support and very practical help to people in crisis and need and work with children, homeless people, all adult victims of modern slavery and those dealing with drug and/or alcohol addiction. Alongside our work in the UK, The Salvation Army International Projects Office works with communities around the world to support and empower them to defeat poverty and injustice. Our development projects are created and implemented in partnership with communities to enable them to build a better life and future for themselves. The Salvation Army is a Christian Church & registered Charity in England (214779), Wales (214779), Scotland (SC009359) and the Republic of Ireland (CHY6399)

The End

Printed in Great Britain
by Amazon

35550675R00085